TURNINGPOINTS

TURNINGPOINTS

Preeminent writers offering fresh, personal
perspectives on the defining events of our time

Published Titles

William Least Heat-Moon, *Columbus in the Americas*
Scott Simon, *Jackie Robinson and the
Integration of Baseball*

Forthcoming Titles

Douglas Brinkley on the March on Washington
William F. Buckley Jr. on the Fall of the Berlin Wall
Eleanor Clift on Passing the 19th Amendment
Thomas Fleming on the Louisiana Purchase
Sir Martin Gilbert on D-Day

America Declares Independence

Also by Alan Dershowitz

*The Abuse Excuse: And Other Cop-outs, Sob Stories,
and Evasion of Responsibility*

The Advocate's Devil: A Novel

The Best Defense

Chutzpah

Contrary to Public Opinion

Criminal Law: Theory and Process
(with Joseph Goldstein and Richard D. Schwartz)

*The Genesis of Justice: Ten Stories of Biblical Injustice
That Led to the Ten Commandments and
Modern Morality and Law*

Just Revenge: A Novel

Letters to a Young Lawyer

Psychoanalysis, Psychiatry, and Law
(with Jay Katz and Joseph Goldstein)

*Reasonable Doubts: The Criminal Justice System
and the O. J. Simpson Case*

Reversal of Fortune: Inside the Von Bülow Case

*Sexual McCarthyism: Clinton, Starr, and
the Emerging Constitutional Crisis*

Shouting Fire: Civil Liberties in a Turbulent Age

*Supreme Injustice: How the High Court
Hijacked Election 2000*

*Taking Liberties: A Decade of Hard Cases,
Bad Laws, and Bum Raps*

*The Vanishing American Jew: In Search of Jewish Identity
for the Next Century*

*Why Terrorism Works: Understanding the Threat,
Responding to the Challenge*

TURNING POINTS

America Declares Independence

ALAN DERSHOWITZ

WILEY

John Wiley & Sons, Inc.

Published by John Wiley & Sons, Inc., Hoboken, New Jersey
Published simultaneously in Canada

Design and production by Navta Associates, Inc.

For general information about our other products and services, please contact our Customer Care Department within the United States at (800) 762-2974, outside the United States at (317) 572-3993 or fax (317) 572-4002.

Wiley also publishes its books in a variety of electronic formats. Some content that appears in print may not be available in electronic books. For more information about Wiley products, visit our web site www.wiley.com.

Library of Congress Cataloging-in-Publication Data:
Dershowitz, Alan M.
    America declares independence / Alan Dershowitz.
        p. cm.
    ISBN 1-63026-029-0
    1. United States. Declaration of Independence.   2. Jefferson, Thomas,
1743–1826—Political and social views.   3. United States. Declaration of
Independence—Criticism, Textual.   I. Title.
    E221 .D47 2003
    973.3'13—dc21

                                                                        2002152554
Printed in the United States of America

10 9 8 7 6 5 4 3 2 1

This book is lovingly dedicated
to my dear departed friends and colleagues
Stephen J. Gould and Robert Nozick,
with whom I taught together for so many years
and on whose intellectual influences
I will always be dependent.

Contents

Acknowledgments

My declaration of dependence on those without whom this book could not have been written includes Eric Citron, who helped me with the historical research; Jane Wagner, who organized my office and typed the manuscript flawlessly; Hana Lane, my editor, who provided excellent editorial input; Helen Rees, my always innovative and caring agent; my family who, as usual, read the manuscript and told me what was wrong with it, and occasionally even what was right with it; and my friends Jeffrey Epstein, Michael and Jackie Halbreich, Stephen Kosslyn, and Rick Paterson for their warm support and inspired suggestions.

Introduction

American independence from Great Britain was achieved on the battlefield, but the establishment of a new republic, conceived in liberty, was as much a product of the pen as the sword. As Thomas Paine, whose own pen contributed to the willingness of colonial Americans to take up the sword, wrote several years after the American Revolution: "[T]he independence of America, considered merely as a separation from England, would have been a matter of but little importance." It became an event worthy of celebration because it was "accompanied by a revolution in the principles and practice of governments."

This book is about the revolution in principles wrought by the pens of American statesmen, rather than the revolution won by the swords and flintlocks of American patriots. Although it is difficult, as a historical matter, to separate the two, my focus will be on the words and ideas used to justify the revolution, and their enduring impact on the "Course of human Events," most particularly the rights of men and women throughout the world.

I have always been intrigued by the Declaration of Independence. Though an important document of liberty, it is a hodgepodge of political, religious, and historical theories. It invokes the laws of nature, as if nature speaks with a single moral voice, and the law of nature's silent God, rather than Christianity's God of revelation. It describes rights as "unalienable" and declares that "all Men are created equal," and yet it presupposes the continued enslavement of men, women, and children who were certainly being denied the unalienable right to liberty "endowed" to them by their Creator. From these natural and God-given rights, the Declaration shifts effortlessly to social contract theory, declaring that governments derive "their just Powers from the Consent of the Governed" rather than from some natural or divine law. The document then moves to a series of alleged wrongs committed against the colonists by the king. Some are profound, such as rendering the military superior to the civil power and denying the benefits of a trial by jury. Some seem trivial, even whiny, such as creating new offices "to harrass our People, and eat out their Substance." Yet other descriptions of wrongs are shameful in their overt racism, such as the reference to "the merciless Indian Savages, whose known Rule of Warfare, is an undistinguished Destruction, of all Ages, Sexes and Conditions." Finally, it invokes the claim of "necessity," then proclaims "a firm Reliance on the Protection of Divine Providence" and pledges the lives, fortunes, and sacred honor of the signers to the cause of independence.

In light of this oft-conflicting rhetoric, it should come as no surprise that its words have been wrenched out of context by partisan pleaders to promote parochial causes. Natural law advocates point to the "Laws of Nature." Libertarians focus on the claim of unalienable rights, especially that of "Liberty." Most recently those who would break down the wall of separation between church and state try to use Thomas Jefferson's own words as battering rams against the structure he himself helped to build. Despite the fact that the Declaration expressly eschewed any mention of the Bible—since some of the most influential of our founding fathers were deists who did not believe in the divine origin of the Bible—modern-day advocates cite the Declaration's invocation of "Nature's God" and "Creator" as proof that we are a Christian or a Judeo-Christian nation founded on Scripture.

In the pages to come, I will examine the various intellectual, religious, and political currents that run through this complex and often misused document of liberty and explore its appropriate place in our structure of government.

This book seeks to reclaim the Declaration for all Americans—indeed, for all people who love liberty and abhor tyranny both of the body and the mind. A review of the history, theology, and political theory underlying the Declaration of Independence will demonstrate that its purpose was not only to provide a justification for our separation from England but also to provide a foundation for a new kind of polity based on "the Consent of the Governed" and, as Jefferson later wrote, the "unbound exercise of reason and freedom of opinion." The Declaration itself was as revolutionary as the course of conduct it sought to justify to "the Opinions of Mankind." Yet we must exercise considerable caution in extrapolating the words of the past to the issues of the present. As I will try to show, the very meanings of words and concepts change markedly with the times. As Oliver Wendell Homes Jr. wisely observed, "a word is not a crystal, transparent and unchanged; it is the skin of a living thought and may vary greatly in color and context according to the circumstances and time in which it is used." Even words as apparently timeless as "God," "nature," "equal," and "rights" convey somewhat different meanings today than they did in 1776.

But first, a brief word about the actual revolution that was the particular subject of the Declaration will place that document in its historical, political, and military setting. The Declaration of Independence, as we all know, was approved on July 4, 1776, but the struggle for independence began well before that iconic date and was to continue for some time thereafter. Historians disagree as to the specific event that marked the beginning of our revolution, since there was no formal declaration of war or any other specific signpost on the long road to separation. Some go back as far as the Boston Massacre of 1770, while others point to the Boston Tea Party in 1773. Most focus on the first actual battle between British soldiers and American patriots, at Lexington and Concord in 1775, where "the shot heard round the world" was fired. The reality is that, as with most complex historical epics, there was no singular event that marked its commencement. The American Revolution was an ongoing process, as the British would surely have argued had they won the war and placed our revolutionaries—from Samuel Adams to James Madison— in the dock for treason.

Among the most prominent defendants would have been those courageous men who evaded British arrest and made it to Philadelphia to attend the First and Second Continental Congresses, in 1775 and 1776. The actual resolution by which the Continental Congress officially voted to separate from Great Britain—the primary overt act of treason—was submitted on June 7, 1776, by Richard Henry Lee (hardly a household name) and was approved on July 2, 1776 (hardly a memorable date). It was an eminently forgettable bare-bones resolution that simply affirmed what everyone already knew to be the fact: that, as Thomas Paine had correctly observed, the period of debate was over and the time had come to declare that "these United Colonies are, and of Right ought to be, Free Independent States, that they are absolved from all Allegiance to the British Crown, and that all political connection between them and the State of Great-Britain is and ought to be totally dissolved."

The Declaration of Independence, approved two days later, was, essentially, an explanation and justification for the action already taken. It was analogous to a judicial opinion delivered several days after the actual judgment had been rendered by a court.

The Continental Congress decided on this bifurcated approach in early June 1776, when, following the introduction of Lee's resolution, it appointed a committee to "prepare a declaration to the effect of the said first resolution."

Thomas Jefferson, John Adams, Benjamin Franklin, Roger Sherman, and Robert Livingston were appointed to serve on the committee. There is some disagreement as to how Jefferson came to draft the Declaration. Adams recalled that Jefferson had proposed that the two of them jointly produce a first draft, but that he deferred to Jefferson because the younger man was a better writer—"you can write ten times better than I can"—and a Virginian. Adams also believed that he himself was "obnoxious, suspected, and unpopular," while Jefferson was "very much otherwise." Jefferson remembered it differently. The committee simply chose him to draft the Declaration: "I consented: I drew it [up]."

There is no disagreement about the fact that Jefferson did compose the first draft and that most of the words of the final document—including its most memorable ones— were his. In his biography of John Adams, David McCullough described the drafting process:

> Alone in his upstairs parlor at Seventh and Market, Jefferson went to work, seated in an unusual revolving Windsor chair and holding on his lap a portable writing box, a small folding desk of his own design which, like the chair, he had specially made for him by a Philadelphia cabinetmaker. Traffic rattled by below the open windows. The June days and nights turned increasingly warm. He worked rapidly and, to judge by surviving drafts, with a sure command of his material. He had none of his books with him, or needed any he later claimed. It was not his objective

to be original, he would explain, only to "place before mankind the common sense of the subject."

In Jefferson's own view, his draft of the Declaration neither aimed at "originality of principle or sentiment, nor yet copied from any particular and previous writing, it was intended to be an expression of the American mind, and to give to that expression the proper tone and spirit called for by the occasion."

While Jefferson was busily writing the words that would help define our new nation—if it were to prevail on the battlefield—George Washington was receiving word that a British fleet of 132 vessels had sailed from Canada and was expected to attack New York. Another 53 warships were approaching Charleston, South Carolina. The most powerful armada and the greatest army ever to reach this continent were poised to attack our cities and seaports. As the historian Joseph J. Ellis reminds us, the members of the Continental Congress were "preoccupied with more pressing military and strategic considerations in the summer of 1776 and did not regard the drafting of the Declaration as their highest priority." But for the man assigned to draft it, nothing could be more important.

Jefferson understood that the immediate purpose of the Declaration was to aid the war effort, both by rallying the troops and in soliciting the support of potential allies. But he had a longer view of the Declaration's ultimate purpose. In a 1826 letter he wrote to the chairman of the 50th anniversary celebration of American independence just days before his own death, Jefferson explained that he

intended the words of the Declaration to be "to the world
. . . the signal of arousing men to burst the chains under
which monkish ignorance and superstition had persuaded
them to bind themselves, and to assume the blessings and
security of self-government." In the ensuing chapters we
will try to understand what Jefferson, and those who
edited and ratified his draft, meant by these ambitious
ideas. We will also see how difficult it is to invoke words
written at one point in history as definitive guides to the
resolution of issues that divide a very different people at a
very different time, and yet how important it is to remain
inspired by the revolutionary spirit that animated these
powerful words and ideas.

1

Who Is the God of the Declaration?

Is He the God of Today's Christian Right?

*I would see no constitutional problem if school-
children were taught the nature of the Founding
Fathers' religious beliefs and how these beliefs
affected the attitudes of the times and the structure of our government.*

—JUSTICE LEWIS POWELL

The Declaration of Independence has been called the birth
certificate of America. In recent years, however, partisans
of the Religious Right have tried to transmogrify this document of liberty into a baptismal certificate for a Christianized America. They point to its invocation of God to
support their sectarian reading of the Declaration.

It is, of course, true that the Declaration proclaims that

"the Laws of Nature and of *Nature's God*" entitle the American people to separate and equal station with their mother country. It also postulates as a self-evident truth that "all Men are created equal [and] are endowed *by their Creator* with certain unalienable Rights" and then appeals to "the *Supreme Judge* of the World." Finally, it expresses "a firm Reliance on the Protection of *Divine Providence.*" (Emphases added in these passages.) It is these references to "Nature's God," "Creator," "Supreme Judge," and "Divine Providence" that have been cited as proof of our founding fathers' commitment to the Judeo-Christian God of the Bible.

For example, Anson Phelps Stokes, the author of a three-volume study of church and state in America published in 1950, argues that Christian values "permeate" the Declaration of Independence. "The ideal of the Declaration is of course a definitely Christian one," especially when "considered along with the references to the Deity." He believes the Declaration is based on "fundamental Christian teachings" including "our duties toward God."

The Reverend Jerry Falwell, the founder of the Moral Majority and now the leader of its successor, the Liberty Federation, has written that "any diligent student of American history finds that our great nation was founded by godly men upon godly principles to be a Christian nation." He goes on to say:

> The Founders actually included their Christian beliefs in their Declaration of Independence. What did they believe?

- They believed in a Creator.

- They believe God created them in His own image.

- They believed that God's supernatural act to create mankind should continue to be extended to every person, which is clearly implied when they wrote "they are endowed by their Creator with certain unalienable rights, that among these are life, liberty and the pursuit of happiness." It is not a stretch to believe that their use of the word "life" implied born and unborn life, black and white life, life for all humans.

- They believed in absolute truth which they called unalienable rights or self-evident truths. The Founders were men of the Bible. They considered this "absolute Truth . . . self-evident Truths."

Similarly, the televangelist and onetime presidential candidate Pat Robertson has characterized our original documents of liberty as designed for "self-government by Christian people." On the basis of this history, he hopes that we will recognize that Jesus:

is Lord of the government, and the church, and business and education, and hopefully, one day, Lord of the press. I see Him involved in everything.

Dr. James Dobson, the head of the conservative group Focus on the Family and a leader of the Religious Right, has observed that:

Given this vast volume of historical evidence, it is utterly foolish to deny that we have been, from the beginning, a people of faith whose government is built wholly on a Judeo-Christian foundation. Yet those of our people who do not study history can be duped into believing anything.

Likewise, the Coral Ridge ministries—an Evangelical group dedicated to "protecting America's Christian heritage by encouraging the application of biblical principles to all spheres of our culture"—distributes glossy pamphlets featuring the Declaration of Independence, along with the message that "antivirtue advocates" who want to remove God and Christianity from public life "have wandered far from the original intent of our founding fathers."

Former vice-presidential candidate Senator Joseph Lieberman also believes that we are a "faith-based" nation, citing the Declaration: "Our rights to life, liberty and the pursuit of happiness [are] based on what our Creator, God, gave us, creating each of us in the image of God." (It is the Bible, however, and not the Declaration that says we are created "in the image of God.")

And during the 1996 presidential campaign, Alan Keyes, who was running for the Republican nomination, argued that the authors of the Declaration of Independence intended it to be "a bridge between the Bible and the Constitution—between the basis of our moral faith and the basis of our political life." Both Keyes and former president George H. W. Bush have said that unless a person believes in the God of the Declaration of Independence, he cannot be a true American. Keyes also has said that the God of the Declaration—"Nature's God"—is not "some mechanistic deity of nature." Rather it is "a very biblical God," a "very personal God." He has started a group called "The Declaration Foundation," whose mission includes the "development of a Declaration curriculum" for use in private and eventually public schools (which he calls "government schools"). The goal of this curriculum would be to persuade schoolchildren that the Declaration of Independence is not based on principles of democracy but rather on the word of God, as revealed by the Bible. He claims that the principles of the Declaration—particularly the references to "creator" and "created"—favor the teaching of *biblical* creationism, which he characterizes as "not religious" but "American." He believes that these principles also support prayer in public schools, while they oppose homosexuality, abortion, and atheism. Keyes also has complained "that I just want to explain to my son Andrew what the Declaration says," namely that by referring to a Creator, it supports biblical creationism. He then goes on to assert: "How dare you stop me," suggesting that anyone in America would try to stop a parent—as distinguished from a public school teacher—from telling his son about creationism.

Nor is this view of the Declaration limited to preachers and politicians. Serious scholars such as Professor Michael Novak have made similar claims. In his 1999 Francis Boyer Lecture, Novak argues that the God of Jefferson's Declaration "is not, and cannot be, a remote watchmaker God." Rather, it is the God of the Bible—the God who "chooses 'chosen' peoples and 'almost chosen peoples'" and "who plays favorites." Novak's biblical God of the Declaration regards us all as fallen "sinners." And Novak apparently believes that Jefferson agreed with the eminent British jurist Sir William Blackstone that "the Law of Moses" is "the font and spring of constitutional government." Novak goes even farther in claiming that by using the words "Creator" and "Nature's God," "Jefferson twice referred to God *in biblical terms*" (emphasis added). Finally, in his most insulting misstatement, he asserts that among the important principles enshrined in the Declaration is one that denies that there can be a "republic," "liberty," or "virtue" "without religion."

A fair reading of the history of the Declaration—and an understanding of the theological and philosophical beliefs of those who drafted it—will prove that virtually every one of the above conclusions, from the ones drawn by Stokes in 1950 to those drawn by Novak in 1999, is demonstrably false.

As I will show in the pages to come, the Declaration was not based on the Bible, and its drafters were most definitely not "men of the Bible." On the contrary, Thomas Jefferson, its primary drafter, believed that the New Testament was written by "ignorant, unlettered men" and that much of it consisted of "so much absurdity, so much untruth, charlatanism and imposture" that it could aptly be characterized as "dung." He thought even less of the Old Testament, whose vengeful God he deplored and whose draconian laws he rejected. He did not believe that the Ten Commandments, with their inclusion of punishment of children for

the sins of their father, came from God, and he characterized the history of the Old Testament as "defective" and
"doubtful." As for the supposed miracles of the Bible, he
compared them to the false miracles of Greek and Roman
mythology. He rejected the "supernatural" and regarded
the concept of the Trinity as "insane." He specifically disagreed with Blackstone's claim that "the Law of Moses" was
the basis of English law, characterizing this claim as a
"fraud" based on an "awkward monkish fabrication." He
even wrote a disquisition against the judicial "usurpation"
that sought to base English governance on "laws made for
the Jews alone, and the precepts of the gospel."

Thomas Jefferson was neither a man of the Bible nor a
person "of faith." He was a man of science and reason. Jefferson abhorred St. Augustine's curse against "the one that
trusteth in Man," for he was one who placed his trust in
human reason over biblical revelation. He rejected the traditional Christian belief that all men were fallen sinners,
and he despised the notion of God having chosen certain
peoples for favorable or unfavorable treatment.

It is difficult to imagine a man less of the Bible than
Thomas Jefferson. Jefferson was an Enlightenment rationalist who believed that "the alliance between church and
state" produces only evil, and that a wall of separation
must be maintained. His God was most certainly not the
intervening Judeo-Christian God of the Bible. It was
"Nature's God"—what the Jefferson scholar Allen Jayne
calls the remote "watchmaker God of deism . . . who
established the laws of nature at the time of creation and
then left it alone."

The last thing he—or John Adams, or Benjamin Franklin—intended was a government "built wholly on a Judeo-Christian foundation." Jefferson railed against such a concept from the moment he penned the Declaration—his next great project was a bill protecting religious freedom in Virginia. And Adams signed a treaty when he was president that explicitly declared that "the government of the United States is not in any sense founded on the Christian religion."

The drafters of our eighteenth-century Declaration of Independence could not have had more different views than those held by today's Falwells, Robertsons, Dobsons, Keyeses, Liebermans, and Novaks. Indeed, as will become evident from a review of the relevant history, Jefferson intended his Declaration to free us not only from the political oppression of Great Britain but also from the religious oppression of evangelical clergymen who elevate "monkish ignorance and superstition" over the "unbound exercise of reason" and "the light of science." He certainly did not accept the insulting notion that there could be no virtue without religion, since he did not care whether anyone, even those closest to him, believed or disbelieved in God, as long as they relied on their own reason, and not the dogma of others, in reaching their decision.

In sum, the Declaration of Independence was designed to protect us from exactly that kind of Christianized America advocated by those who are now seeking to hijack the Declaration for their own sectarian purposes. The prominent historian Pauline Maier has put it this way: "As the heirs of a political tradition shaped by radical seventeenth-century English Protestants, most American revolutionaries were suspicious of Roman Catholicism and its iconographic traditions. Many went further and opposed the use of religion to reinforce the power of the state in any way: Indeed, separation of church and state was one of the most radical innovations of the American Revolution."

Jefferson's Nonbiblical God of Nature

The Judeo-Christian God—Jehovah of the Old Testament and the Father of Jesus in the New Testament—was *not* the God Thomas Jefferson was referring to as Nature's God or the Creator. Jefferson explicitly rejected the biblical God— "the Lord mighty in battle," the God who intervened in the lives of human beings, performed miracles, wrote the Bible, or had a son. Jefferson did not believe in divine revelation, the virgin birth, the Trinity, or the other fundamental theological underpinnings of Christianity. According to the historian Allen Jayne, the author of a recent, definitive study on Jefferson's theology, Jefferson rejected "orthodox Christian doctrine" and "before and during the time he drafted the Declaration of Independence, manifested a concealed 'hatred for ceremonial institutionalized Christianity.'" Nor did he believe that Jesus was anything other than an ordinary human being or that Moses received the Ten Commandments from God. Jefferson's "watchmaker" God did not answer human prayers.

Most importantly, although Jefferson's words are currently invoked by "people of faith"—as members of the
Religious Right refer to themselves—Jefferson himself
was the opposite of a person of faith. He rejected all
reliance on conventional religious notions of "faith" based
on revelation, miracles, or dogma. These concepts were
anathema to him. Instead, he insisted that "human reason"
was supreme, and if a person could not be convinced of a
fact—including the existence of God—by reason alone, he
should not accept that fact on the basis of faith, revelation,
or dogma. In 1787 he wrote about the study of religion to
his seventeen-year-old nephew Peter Carr, to whom he was
proposing a complete course of study. Because this letter
outlines Jefferson's views on religion perhaps more completely than any other single document, it warrants extensive quotation:

> Your reason is now mature enough to examine this
> object [religion]. In the first place, divest yourself of
> all bias in favor of novelty and singularity of opinion.
> On the other hand, shake off all the fears and servile
> prejudices, under which weak minds are servilely
> crouched. Fix reason firmly in her seat, and call to her
> tribunal every fact, every opinion. *Question with bold-
> ness even the existence of God; because, if there be one, he
> must more approve of the homage of reason, than that of
> blindfolded fear.* You will naturally examine first, the
> religion of your own country. Read the Bible, then, as
> you would read Livy or Tacitus. The facts which are
> within the ordinary course of nature, you will believe

on the authority of the writer, as you do those of the same kind in Livy and Tacitus. The testimony of the writer weighs in their favor, in one scale, and their not being against the laws of nature, does not weigh against them. But those facts in the Bible which contradict the laws of nature, must be examined with more care, and under a variety of faces. Here you must recur to the pretensions of the writer to inspiration from God. Examine upon what evidence his pretensions are founded, and whether that evidence is so strong, as that its falsehood would be more improbable than a change in the laws of nature, in the case he relates. For example, in the book of Joshua, we are told, the sun stood still several hours. Were we to read that fact in Livy of Tacitus, we should class it with the showers of blood, speaking of statues, beasts, etc. But it is said, that the writer of that book was inspired. Examine, therefore, candidly, evidence there is of his having been inspired. The pretension is entitled to your inquiry, because millions believe it. On the other hand, you are astronomer enough to know how contrary it is to the law of nature that a body revolving on its axis, as the earth does, should have stopped, should not, by that sudden stoppage, have prostrated animals, trees, buildings, and should after a certain time have resumed its revolution, and that without a second general prostration. Is this arrest of the earth's motion, or the evidence which affirms it, most within the law of probabilities? You would next read the New

Testament. It is a history of a personage called Jesus.
Keep in your eye the opposite pretensions: 1, of those
who say he was begotten by God, born of a virgin,
suspended and reversed the laws of nature at will, and
ascended bodily into heaven; and 2, of those who say
he was a man of illegitimate birth, of a benevolent
heart, enthusiastic mind, who set out without pretensions to divinity, ended in believing them, and was
punished capitally for sedition, by being gibbeted,
according to the Roman law, which punished the first
commission of that offence by whipping, and the second by exile, or death *in fureu*. . . .

Do not be frightened from this inquiry by any fear of
its consequences. If it ends in a belief that there is no
God, you will find incitements to virtue in the comfort
and pleasantness you feel in its exercise, and the love of
others which it will procure you. If you find reason to
believe there is a God, a consciousness that you are
acting under his eye, and that he approves you, will
be a vast additional incitement, if there be a future
state, the hope of a happy existence in that increases
the appetite to deserve it; if that Jesus was also a God,
you will be comforted by a belief of his aid and love.
In fine, I repeat, you must lay aside all prejudice on
both sides, and neither believe nor reject anything,
because any other persons, or description of persons,
have rejected or believed it. *Your own reason is the*
only oracle given you by Heaven, and you are answer-
able, not for the rightness, but the uprightness of the
decision. [Emphases added.]

It is impossible to conclude from this letter—in which Jefferson tells his own nephew that he would "find incitements to virtue" in "a belief that there is no God"—that Jefferson was among those self-righteous religious bigots who suggest that a person without religion cannot be virtuous. Indeed, in drafting his bill for establishing religious freedom in Virginia, Jefferson wrote that "our civil rights have no dependence on our religious opinions any more than our opinions in physics or geometry." Just as no one could rationally argue that one's views on geometry bear any relationship to one's virtue, it followed for Jefferson that one's views on God bear no relationship to one's virtue as well.

The letter also demonstrates that Jefferson rejected Pascal's cynical wager—that it is a better bet to believe in a nonexistent God than to risk damnation from an existing one—as well as the anti-intellectual God who would reward a crass cost-benefit analysis that led to "belief" in Him, while punishing an honest inquiry that led to skepticism or disbelief. Just as no God worthy of respect would punish a person for not believing in Euclidean geometry, so, too, no just God would punish a thinking person for not believing in Him. I could never comprehend the justice or rationality of any religious view that limited salvation—or any kind of religious reward—to those who believe in God or a particular savior. If there is a God and he is just, he must reward those who honestly struggle with the mystery of his existence and arrive at the "wrong" answer, as Jefferson believed. Life cannot be a betting parlor with heaven as payoff for winning a wager.

Jefferson believed that a certain level of maturity was required for the objective study of religion. Accordingly, he opposed Bible study or reading by young students, arguing in his *Notes on the State of Virginia* that "instead . . . of putting the Bible and Testament into the hands of the children at an age when their judgments are not sufficiently matured for religious enquiries, their memories may be stored with the most useful facts from Grecian, Roman, European and American history." He feared that young students would be subjected to religious indoctrination rather than the kind of open inquiry he thought essential to the study of religion.

Jefferson's own personal belief in a nonintervening God of nature was the product of his reasoning and his evaluation of the evidence available during the late eighteenth and early nineteenth centuries (just as his "suspicion" that blacks were inherently mentally inferior to whites was based on his reason and his limited experience as a slaveowner). He was willing to be persuaded that he was wrong as to these, and other, beliefs.

Jefferson's Rejection of "Faith" and "Revelation" in Favor of "Human Reason" and "Experience"

To Thomas Jefferson, the important distinction was not between those who believed in God and those who did not. The important difference, as he explained to his nephew, was between those who arrived at their conclusion regarding God by human reason rather than by "faith," "dogma," "revelation," or other "unscientific" or "super- natural" means. Jefferson, along with most of his intellec- tual mentors and peers, rejected what Thomas Paine referred to in *The Age of Reason* as the "imaginary thing called faith." Instead, they observed the available evidence and employed their own reason to conclude that God, in fact, existed. For them, belief in God did not require, or even permit, a "leap of faith." It required a scientific inquiry, governed by reason, into the factual support for God's existence. Indeed, for some deists, the existence of God was more a matter of logic than science. For them, God was a product of a syllogism: The universe exists; it must have been created; if it was created, there must have been an original creator; we call that original creator by the name of God. "We are"—they reason—"therefore He must be." Yet Jefferson maintained that if another person's inquiry led that person to the opposite conclusion, he should follow his reasoning and not believe in God. Unlike Augustine, Jefferson trusted "in man."

Throughout his life, Jefferson elevated human *reason* over dogmatic *belief,* even—perhaps especially—belief in God. In his intellectual world, there was a null hypothesis that posited the nonexistence of God if evidence and human reason lead to that conclusion. The Jefferson biog- rapher Willard Sterne Randall writes that he had an "uncompromising belief in reason as the sole and final arbiter of knowledge and worth." His early education and extensive reading had "liberated him from faith," according to Jayne, who wrote that "To him it was not sufficient to state 'I believe' and merely recite religious opinions without any rational justification. Such affirmations were the method of faith, and Jefferson, as an advocate of reason, thought that religious opinion should be justified by arguments born of reason." This is the mind-set of the scientist and the skeptic, not the man of faith in divine revelation.

To many of his contemporaries, Jefferson's mind-set was also that of the "infidel," the "apostate," and the "heretic." During Jefferson's first campaign for the presidency, his opponents declared him to be an "atheist" and argued that a vote for Jefferson was, as his contemporary the Reverend William Linn put it, "no less than a rebellion against God." As proof of Jefferson's atheism, his own words of toleration from the *Notes on the State of Virginia* were thrown back at him. There he had said, damningly in the minds of his detractors, "it does me no injury for my neighbor to say there are twenty gods, or no God."

Jefferson as a "Man of the Bible"

As further proof of Jefferson's atheism, his disbelief in the alleged miracles recounted in the Bible was cited. Jefferson had "doubted the reality of the flood" and had "sinned in questioning the age of the earth." He had even compared the supernatural myths of Christianity with those of the ancient Greeks and Romans, predicting that:

the day will come when the mystical generation of Jesus by the Supreme Being as His Father, in the womb of a virgin, will be classed with the fable of the generation of Minerva in the brain of Jupiter.*

Jefferson not only disbelieved specific "mystical" accounts in the Bible, he also rejected "the mystical and metaphysical elements in Christianity, which he attributed to Plato's fuzzy thinking."

Jefferson apparently derived many of his views about the Bible from other deists, and he shared many of Thomas Paine's criticisms of both the Old and the New Testaments. Paine—who was famous throughout the colonies for writing *Common Sense,* the pamphlet that helped inspire the revolution—also wrote *The Age of Reason,* a widely read book that savaged the Bible as a "pious fraud." Jefferson's analogy between biblical miracles and earlier mythological fables is similar to Paine's, who had based much of his criticism on the work of earlier deists. Paine repeatedly compared the miracles of the Bible to the supernatural accounts contained in Greek and Roman mythology. Indeed, he argued—quite persuasively—that the stories in the New Testament were, in fact, copied from earlier "heathen" accounts. Paine wrote of the virgin birth that: "This story is upon the face of it, the same kind of story of Jupiter and Ledia and Jupiter and Europa or any of the amorous adventures of Jupiter; and shows . . . that the Christian faith is built upon the heathen mythology."

---

*He probably would have approved also of Keith Preston's doggerel:
The great god Ra, whose shrine once covered acres,
is filler now for crossword puzzle makers.

Paine went on to explain why Christians were prepared to believe the supernatural account of Jesus' birth:

It is, however, not difficult to account for the credit that was given to the story of Jesus Christ being the Son of god. He was born at a time when the heathen mythology had still some fashion and repute in the world, and that mythology had prepared the people for the belief of such a story. Almost all the extraordinary men that lived under the heathen mythology were reputed to be some of the sons of their gods. It was not a new thing, at that time, to believe a man to have been celestially begotten: the intercourse of gods with women was then a matter of familiar opinion. Their Jupiter according to their accounts, had cohabited with hundreds; the story therefore, had nothing in it neither new, wonderful, or obscene; it was conformable to opinions that then prevailed among the people called Gentiles or Mythologists and it was these people only that believed it. The Jews who had kept strictly to the belief in one God and who had always rejected the heathen mythology never credited the story. [Paine was not quite accurate. The Old Testament, in fact, contains stories about gods mating with humans. See Genesis 5:4.]

Paine concluded, therefore, that "the theory of what is called the Christian church sprung out of the tail of heathen mythology." He argued that "a direct incorporation took place in the first instance by making the reputed founder celestially begotten." He also believed that the

> trinity of gods that then followed was no other than a reduction of the former plurality. . . . The statue of Mary succeeded the statue of Diana of Ephesus. The deification of heroes changed into the canonization of saints. The Mythologists had gods for everything: the Christian Mythologists had saints for everything; the church became as crowded with the one as the Pantheon had been with the other, and Rome was the place of both.

Paine's ultimate conclusion was a scathing attack on the Christian church: "Of all the systems of religion that ever were invented, there is none more derogatory to the Almighty, more unedifying to man, more repugnant to reason, and more contradictory in itself, than this thing called Christianity. Too absurd for belief, too impossible to convince, and too inconsistent for practice, it renders the heart torpid, or produces only atheists and fanatics. As an engine of power, it serves the purpose of despotism; and as a means of wealth, the avarice of priests; but so far as respects the good of man in general, it leads to nothing here or hereafter." He continued: "The Christian theory is little else than idolatry of the ancient Mythologists; accommodated to the purpose of power and revenue; and it yet remains to reason and philosophy to abolish the amphibious fraud." He concluded that "the Bible and the

Testament are impositions on the world, that the fall of man, the account of Jesus Christ being the Son of God, and of his dying to appease the wrath of God, and of salvation by that strange means, are all fabulous inventions and dishonorable to the wisdom and power of Almighty."

Paine and many of the other deists had similar criticisms of the Old Testament, a book that Paine regarded as "spurious." He was even critical of the Ten Commandments, which he argued "carry no internal evidence of divinity within them." He acknowledged that they contain some good moral precepts, "such as any man qualified to be a lawgiver or a legislator, could produce himself, without having recourse to supernatural intervention." But as to one provision contained in the Ten Commandments— "that God visits the sins of the father upon the children"— Paine argued that "it is contrary to every principle of moral justice."

Jefferson also disbelieved in the divine origin of the Ten Commandments, asking in an 1824 letter to John Adams:

> Where did we get the ten commandments? The book indeed give them to us verbatim, but where did it get them? For itself tells us they were written by the finger of God on tables of stone, which were destroyed by Moses; it specifies those on the second set of tables in different form and substance, but still without saying how the other were recovered. But the whole history of these books is so defective and doubtful, that it seems vain to attempt minute inquiry into it; and such tricks have been played

with their text, and with the other texts of other books relating to them, that we have a right from that cause to entertain much doubt what parts of them are genuine.

Jefferson had special contempt for the writers of the Gospels, whom he considered to be "ignorant, unlettered men." He regarded these writers as impostors, false witnesses, and corrupters of the true teachings of Jesus. He described "the stupidity of some, and roguery of other of His disciples." He characterized the descriptions of Jesus' life as "a groundwork of vulgar ignorance, of things impossible, of superstitions, fanaticism, and fabrications." He found it hard to believe that the Gospels, which contained "so much ignorance, so much absurdity, so much untruth, charlatanism and imposture," could have come from "the same being" who wrote the moral portions of these books. The words of Jesus he called "diamonds," and the words of his disciples he called "dung." According to Jaroslav Pelikan, a leading scholar in the history of Christianity, it was Jefferson's view that "the real villain in the Christian story was the apostle Paul, who had corrupted the religion of Jesus into a religion about Jesus, which thus had, in combination with the otherworldly outlook of the Fourth gospel produced the monstrosities of dogma, superstition, and priest craft, which were the essence of Christian orthodoxy." Jefferson believed that Jesus was "the greatest of all the reformers of the depraved religion of his own country," and that Paul was the "first corrupter of the doctrines of Jesus."

Jefferson's Views of Jesus and "Christ"

Although he considered himself a Christian—in the sense of approving of many of Jesus' *human* qualities—Jefferson, in fact, disagreed with the core of his religious and moral teachings. Here is how Jefferson himself put it: "It is not to be understood that I am with him in all his doctrines. I am a Materialist; he takes the side of Spiritualism. He preaches the efficacy of repentance towards the forgiveness of sin; I require a counterpoise of good works to redeem it, etc., etc." Jefferson also regarded himself as "an Epi- curean." He considered the "genuine . . . doctrines of Epicurus as containing everything rational in moral philosophy which Greece and Rome left us." Epicurus preached that "pleasure is the beginning and end of the blessed life"—a very un-Christian notion. Jefferson agreed, saying "that a hedonistic 'pursuit of happiness' was not inconsistent with an 'innate moral sense,'" and he himself lived a life of both reflection and hedonism, one that even- tually drove him to the brink of bankruptcy.

In addition to disagreeing with Jesus' central doctrines of spirituality and redemption, Jefferson made it clear that he explicitly rejected "the immaculate conception of Jesus, His deification, the creation of the world by Him, His miraculous powers, His resurrection and visible ascension, His corporal Presence in the Eucharist, the Trinity, original sin, atonement, regeneration, election, Orders of Hierar- chy, etc." He had particular disdain for the concept of the

Trinity, characterizing it as "incomprehensible, unintelligible and insane." He revered the writings of Joseph Priestley, who argued that the Trinity was a corruption based on a comparison between Jesus as the Son of God and "Mercury, Jupiter's Son." Jefferson did not believe "in the existence of the traditional Christian heaven and hell," in the concept of "being saved," or in "grace." He was "influenced by the Roman stoics to view suicide with sympathy," despite the Christian prohibition against taking one's own life. Most importantly, "it was a prime article of Jefferson's deistic religion that Jesus was not a deity." In other words, Jefferson rejected all the central tenants of orthodox Christianity.

Indeed, it took some courage for Jefferson to express these heretical views, since under Virginia law, heresy was a serious crime. Any person raised as a Christian who denied the Trinity or the divine authority of Scripture could be disqualified from holding office, and even have his children taken away and placed into more orthodox hands.

Beyond this, Jefferson's skepticism regarding Christianity was not limited to its supernatural aspects. Although he admired the teachings of Jesus, he did not believe that Jesus' philosophy, which was scattered through the Gospels, was anything more than an "unconnected system of ethics," which were "defective as a whole." He contrasted the teachings of Jesus with the "writings of ancient heathen moralists," which he believed would be "more full, more entire, more coherent, and more clearly deduced from unquestionable principles of knowledge."

Was Jefferson Even a Christian?

Jefferson rarely attended church and he viewed "the priest"—broadly defined to encompass all clerics—as "always in alliance with the despot, abetting his abuses in return for protection to his own." He despised the sectarianism of the Christian churches: "You may ask my opinion on the items of doctrine in your catechism. I have never permitted myself to mediate a specified creed. These formulas have been the bane and ruin of the Christian church, its own fatal invention, which, through so many ages, made of Christendom a slaughter-house, and at this day divides it into castes of inextinguishable hatred to one another."

Yet despite his rejection of Christian dogma, Jefferson declared himself to be a Christian "in the only sense he [Jesus] wished anyone to be; sincerely attached to his doctrines in preference to all others; ascribing to himself every *human* excellence; and believing he never claimed any other" (emphasis added). In other words, he accepted *Jesus* (at least in part) while rejecting *Christ* (in every respect). It is difficult, therefore, to accept his claim to being a Christian, since the very word connotes acceptance of Jesus as the "Christos," the divinely anointed Messiah. In some of his private correspondence, he distinguished between deists like himself, on the one hand, and Christians, on the other. It is likely that he publicly embraced the word "Christianity" for expedient political reasons, while rejecting its theological essence, for personal philosophical reasons. His critics called him an "opposer of Christianity," a man who had "a total disregard to public worship and an absolute indifference to religion whatsoever."

Would Jefferson Today Be Considered a "Secular Humanist" or a "Unitarian"?

Several of Jefferson's biographers have speculated about where Jefferson's views on religion would place him in today's world of religious categories. Jefferson variously considered himself a Christian, a deist, and a Unitarian. In 1822 he wrote the following:

> I rejoice that in this blessed country of free enquiry and belief, which has surrendered its creed and conscience to neither kings nor priests, the genuine doctrine of one only God is reviving, and I trust there is not a young man now living in the United States who will not die an Unitarian.

Jayne wrote of Jefferson's possible Unitarianism that it

> was not only in accord with the use of individual critical reason in religion as espoused and put into practice by the Enlightenment and Jefferson; it was a product of the Enlightenment and critical reason. It would seem, therefore, that Jefferson regarded it as the religious counterpart of the University of Virginia, which Charles Sanford described as "an institution

that would foster the development of the ideals of the enlightenment by which he had lived all his life." Indeed, Unitarianism was perceived by Jefferson as a religion that corresponded generally with the theology of the Declaration of Independence and one that, like that theology, was conductive to the efficacy of the political theory of the document. As a religion based on individual reasons and judgment, it served and preserved the similarly based politics of the Declaration.

Whether Unitarianism—which rejects much of Christian theological dogma—can be considered a Christian religion remains a hotly debated issue.

The biographer Joseph Ellis has said that "in modern day parlance, he was a secular humanist"—a term of opprobrium to those of the contemporary Religious Right, who cite the words of his Declaration in support of their fundamentalist agenda. He has been described as an Enlightenment rationalist, a religious skeptic, and a scientific believer in God by design. He also has been called a secularist and even the father of "the secularization of scientific research in America." His political enemies accused him of being an infidel, especially since he continued to praise Thomas Paine even after Paine wrote his vitriolic attack on the Bible and Christianity in *The Age of Reason*. "Federalist newspaper editors had a field day describing 'the two Toms' walking arm in arm, allegedly comparing notes on the ideal way to promote atheism or their past successes in despoiling Christian virgins." Dozens of pamphlets and articles characterized Jefferson as a "French infidel and atheist." Alexander Hamilton, who himself had little use for religion, called Jefferson an "atheist and fanatic." Writings by and about Jefferson were banned from the Philadelphia public library until 1830 on the ground of his purported atheism. Even many years later, President Theodore Roosevelt attacked Paine as "a filthy little atheist." But neither Jefferson nor Paine were atheists. They both accepted the God of Nature while rejecting the God of Judaism, Christianity, and Islam. Indeed, they viewed deism as a true religion capable of saving the world from the kind of atheistic reaction to Christianity that was being seen in France. Paine's justification for penning *The Age of Reason* was that he "was genuinely alarmed by the growth of atheism and was convinced that the growing disbelief in God and a future life was due primarily to the disgust men felt for the reactionary and rigid conduct of the clergy."

Although Jefferson considered himself religious, he would not be so considered by some of today's religious thinkers. The Yale law professor Stephen Carter, for example, defines religion as "the belief in supernatural intervention in human affairs." Such belief, according to Carter, "is a useful divider" because "this is where the culture seems to draw the line." There can be no question about on which side of that dividing line Jefferson's views fall.

Did Jefferson Believe
in an Afterlife?

The reality is that Thomas Jefferson's views of religion were a hodgepodge of Enlightenment rationality, deism by design, political opportunism, and contradictions. They also changed over time, especially after he was attacked for being an atheist. One example of his contradictory theology lies in his belief in life after death, despite there being as little evidence for that conclusion as for the virgin birth, the resurrection, or the divine origin of the Ten Commandments. Yet life after death was a firm tenet of much of the deism of the day, even that of Thomas Paine, who wrote, "I hope for happiness beyond this life." Paine's "scientific" arguments for an afterlife are embarrassingly unscientific:

> I content myself with believing, even to positive conviction, that the Power that gave me existence is able to continue it, in any form and manner He pleases, either with or without this body . . .
> . . . A very numerous part of the animal creation preaches to us, far better than Paul, the belief of a life hereafter. Their little life resembles an earth and a heaven—a present and a future state, and comprises, if it may be so expressed, immortality in miniature.
> The most beautiful parts of the creation to our eye are the winged insects, and they are not so originally. They acquire that form and that inimitable bril-

liancy by progressive changes. The slow and creeping caterpillar-worm of to-day passes in a few days to a torpid figure and a state resembling death; and in the next change comes forth in all the miniature magnificence of life, a splendid butterfly.

No resemblance of the former creature remains; everything is changed; all his powers are new, and life is to him another thing. We cannot conceive that the consciousness of existence is not the same in this state of the animal as before; why then must I believe that the resurrection of the same body is necessary to continue to me the consciousness of existence hereafter?

Confusing metaphor with science, Paine hoped for a metamorphosis from his earthly body to some new form of existence in the hereafter.

What Paine merely hoped for, Jefferson seemed to accept, especially as he grew older. He repeatedly wrote to friends that "we [shall] meet again in another place." Some Jefferson scholars argue that his statements about an afterlife suggest approval of the concept as a practical spur to good deeds—"the great sanction"—rather than as an actual belief: "As a student of law and history and a practicing attorney and statesman, he saw the importance of a belief in eternal judgment for encouraging a moral life of service to society." Thus Jefferson's afterlife did not reward or punish based on "faith which is not within our power," but instead on "our good works which are within our power."

If Jefferson's acceptance of an afterlife as a reward for good works was more a tactical way of encouraging good behavior than a deeply felt belief, he was certainly not alone—then or today. Many agnostics and atheists accept religion because they believe it does some good, even if it is based on a pious fraud. The case for religion as placebo is persuasive to many decent people. If others believe in God, an afterlife, or the efficacy of prayer, this set of beliefs may be beneficial to them, even if it turns out to be untrue. So why try to disabuse them of their false, though beneficial, beliefs? This approach to religion, or an afterlife, is akin to Pascal's wager: It is better to believe than to disbelieve in God, because if He does not exist and you believe He does, you have risked nothing, but if you do not believe in Him and He does exist, you will be punished in the afterlife (provided, of course, that God punishes you for your ultimate beliefs, even if they are the product of a cost-benefit calculation, rather than for your honest efforts to find the truth). Religion as placebo is less cynical than Pascal's wager but equally tactical.

There is also the related question of whether religion (or belief in God) is good or bad for society, regardless of whether it is "true" or "false." Even if every aspect of a given religion is totally bogus, the religion can produce much good, as the "false" religions of Greek, Roman, and Egyptian mythology did. The literature, art, philosophy, and architecture inspired by these "false" religions are every bit as great as those inspired by "true" religions. The religiously inspired music of Bach is as beautiful whether God exists or not, or whether Jesus is or is not the Savior. I get emotional every time I listen to the finale of Verdi's Requiem, even though I (and Verdi) believe not a word of its text.

There are various conclusions a rational person can reach about religion, among which are the following:

- It is true and produces good.
- It is true and produces bad or mixed results.
- It is false and produces good.
- It is false and produces bad or mixed results.
- It cannot be known whether it is true, but it can be known that it produces good, bad, or mixed results.

Jefferson seemed to conclude that belief in God was true and produced good results, that belief in the supernatural and institutional aspects of organized religion is false and produces bad results, and that belief in reward and punishment after death is unprovable but produces good results—if judgment is based on deeds rather than beliefs.

Jefferson often wrote of the "pillow of ignorance" on which he was willing to rest his uncertain brain when it came to issues about which people could not be sure, including life after death. Jefferson saw Jesus' promise of life after death as a major improvement over what he mistakenly believed was the Jewish view. "He [Jesus], taught, emphatically, the doctrines of a future state, which was either doubted or disbelieved by the Jews; and wheedled it with efficacy, as an important incentive, supplementary to the other motives to moral conduct." Jefferson was correct about biblical Judaism, but he was apparently ignorant of rabbinic Judaism, which for several hundred years before the birth of Jesus had insisted on life after death. Indeed, Jefferson's critique of Judaism as lacking concern for humanity as a whole was ignorant of the writings of Jesus' predecessors such as Rabbi Hillel, who foreshadowed many of Jesus' statements about the love of all humanity. Hillel, some years before Jesus, had famously responded to the challenge to teach the whole Pentateuch standing on one leg by saying: "That which is despicable to you, do not do to your fellow, this is the whole Torah, and the rest is commentary." Jefferson was thus apparently unaware that Jesus was expressing a traditional Jewish view when he wrote, "To love God with all thy heart and thy neighbor as thyself is the sum of religion." Indeed, if Jesus was neither the son of God nor a supernatural figure of any kind—as Jefferson firmly believed he was not—then an apt characterization of this great human being is that he was the first Reform rabbi, a Jew who rejected much of the ritualistic aspects of traditional Judaism in favor of its more spiritual and ethical teachings, which he elaborated, adapted, and extended. Jefferson might well have been comfortable with such a characterization of the very human Jesus in whose teachings he believed.

Jefferson's "Argument by Design" for the Existence of Nature's God

Jefferson's argument for God "by the design of nature" is popular today among fundamentalists who seek to use science to prove the existence of God. This is how Jefferson explained his scientific approach to John Adams:

I hold, (without appeal to revelation) that when we take a view of the universe, in its parts, general or particular, it is impossible for the human mind not to perceive and feel a conviction of design, consummate skill, and indefinite power in every atom of its composition. The movements of the heavenly bodies, so exactly held in their course by the balance of centrifugal and centripetal forces; the structure of our earth itself, with its distribution of lands, waters and atmosphere; animal and vegetable bodies, examined in all their minutest particles; insects, mere atoms of life, yet as perfectly organized as man or mammoth; . . . it is impossible, I say, for the human mind not to believe, that there is in all this, design, cause and effect, up to an ultimate cause, a Fabricator of all things from matter and motion.

David Hume had earlier responded to the "argument by design" in the following way:

Look around this universe. What an immense profusion of beings, animated and organized, sensible and active! You admire this prodigious variety and fecundity. But inspect a little more narrowly these living existences. . . . How hostile and destructive to each other! . . . The whole presents nothing but the idea of a blind nature, impregnated by a great vivifying principle, and pouring fourth from her lap, without discernment or parental care, her maimed and abortive children.

A century later, Darwin was to provide a systematic scientific basis for Hume's observation.

In my book *Shouting Fire* I elaborate on Hume's argument as follows:

> The reality is that nature is morally neutral. It is full of beauty and wonder, but it thrives on violence and predation. Nature is a mother animal nursing her helpless cub and then killing another helpless animal to survive. Nature is life-giving sunshine followed by death-dealing floods. Human nature is Albert Schweitzer and Adolf Hitler, Jesus and Torquemada, Kant and Nietzsche, Confucius and Pol Pot, Mandela and bin Laden, the early Martin Luther, who reached out to the despised, and the later Martin Luther, who advocated rounding up the Jews and making them "miserable captives" in forced-labor camps.
>
> In constructing a moral code—or a system of rights—one should not ignore the varieties of human nature, or their alleged commonalities. But neither can the diverse components of nature be translated directly into morality, legality, or rights. The complex relationship between the *is* of nature and the *ought* of morality must be mediated by human experience.

For honest proponents of the "argument by design"— those who seek the objective truth wherever it may take them, rather than those who seek to "prove" an already accepted premise—the conclusion may change over time. The "argument by design" is an argument of exclusion: There *must* be a god, because there is no *other* plausible explanation for the benign design of the world. As Prat de Lamartine was to put it several generations after Jefferson: "God—but a word invoked to explain the world." Indeed, it is uncertain whether Jefferson and his fellow deists would have arrived at their deistic conclusion if they were aware of current scientific explanations of how the world came about. In the wake of the discoveries of Darwin, Einstein, and others, many deists became agnostics or atheists. That is the "danger" of the "argument by design" and why so many people of faith reject it as dangerous: It makes belief in God dependent on the progress of science in filling in gaps, rendering it decreasingly likely that God is needed as science explains more and more. The God of design is the diminishing God of the diminishing gaps. Although there will always be gaps in our collective knowledge of the universe—we are all "Newton's dog" when it comes to the origin of matter—we now understand that the existence of these gaps is itself explainable by science. It is not surprising that deism and belief in the God of Nature reached its peak after Galileo and Newton and began to decline after Darwin and Einstein.

For Jefferson, belief in the existence of Nature's God did not require a leap of faith; the real "leap"—to Jefferson, an irrational and illogical one—would be from God's existence to his authorship of the Bible, his revelation to selected humans, his performing of miracles, and his need for churches, prayers, and priests. There is nothing in the design of the world that could possibly lead a rational person to believe that God wrote a deeply flawed book filled with injustice, falsehoods, and unnatural occurrences. Indeed, if design *proved* God's existence, that same design—and the laws of nature governing it—would tend to disprove claims of supernatural, miraculous, and unobservable phenomena. Jefferson characterized the intervening Judeo-Christian God of miracles as "a bungling artist" who could not get it right in the first place. A true God would create rules of nature that did not require the help of supernatural miracles. Nor would a perfect God demand that people believe in him or build churches or establish religious hierarchies to worship him. He would judge each person, as Jefferson told his nephew, "not for the rightness" of his beliefs, but for the "uprightness" and honesty of the rational process by which it was reached.

Ultimately all scientific, empirical, or logical arguments for God's existence must fail under the accepted rules of science, empiricism, and logic. The only plausible argument for God is an unscientific, antiempirical, and illogical reliance on blind (deaf and dumb) *faith*—precisely the sort of faith Jefferson rejected. Pope Gregory I was wiser than Jefferson when he said, "If the work of God could be comprehended by reason, it would be no longer wonderful, and faith would have no merit if reason provided proof." The critics of deism were right as a matter of empirical truth when they predicted that deism would inevitably lead to agnosticism (though that word had not yet been coined) and atheism. Paine and Jefferson were wrong in believing that deism would save religion from atheism. Any belief in God that is based on science, empiricism, and logic will eventually lead to doubt about or disbelief in God. Indeed, any religious claim that purports to be provable or disprovable by the canons of science—whether it is deism, creationism, literal belief in miracles, or the end of the world at a predicted time—will end up in the wastebin of history, along with the geocentric theory, the authenticity of the Shroud of Turin, and the Bible Codes. Science will never prove religion to be true, and if religion submits its empirical claims to scientific proof, it will prove them false. As our knowledge gap narrows, belief in God's existence can survive only if it lays claims to a magisterium outside of science, and many contemporary religious leaders understand this far better than Jefferson did. Jefferson was naive in believing that science and rationality could discover God or prove his existence, because the object of science is to explain every phenomenon without recourse to the supernatural, the unempirical, or the illogical. The deus ex machina is outside of science. The most that science can ever say is "we can explain this" or "we cannot yet explain that." It cannot take the next step—as Jefferson tried to do—and say, "since we cannot explain it, it must be the work of a God" or some other supernatural phenomenon outside the magisterium of science. Individual scientists may, of course, accept faith and believe in God without trying to prove God's existence scientifically. But in his effort to replace faith and revelation with rationality and science, Jefferson laid the foundation for skepticism, agnosticism, and secularism—even if that was not his intention.

In a class I teach at Harvard that deals with religion, science, philosophy, and law, I try to test the proposition—rejected by Jefferson but espoused by my late colleague Stephen Jay Gould and my coteacher Harvey Cox—that religion and science occupy separate magesteria: that the former deals with normative issues of morality, while the latter deals with empirical issues of fact. I try to challenge the sharpness of this separation by arguing that for many religious people, their "faith" is actually based on the empirical conclusion that certain "events"—which are central to their religion—actually took place. I pose two hypothetical scenarios to the students who profess faith in the Christian, Jewish, or Muslim religions. The first posits a camera on a galaxy several thousand light-years away that can send images back to earth much faster than the speed of light—in fact, instantaneously. The camera is focused on Sinai, Calvary, and the Dome of the Rock, and proves to the complete empirical satisfaction of the students that no Ten Commandments were given to Moses on Sinai, that Jesus was not resurrected, and that Muhammad did not ascend to heaven with his horse.

The second hypothetical scenario asks students to imagine that they are on a "dig" in the Qumran Caves outside of Jerusalem, where the original Dead Sea Scrolls were discovered. In a distant part of a previously unexplored cave, one of the students discovers a new scroll sealed in a jug. He has with him a machine capable of determining the age and authenticity of the scroll. It proves to be authentic. He opens it up and reads it in the original language. It is the proceedings of a conclave of ancient priests who are trying to get their people to be more moral and law-abiding. They discuss various options, and the high priest comes up with the idea of staging an event on top of a mountain at which a man dressed up to look like God gives another man, posing as a prophet, two tablets containing Ten Rules of Conduct. "The people will have to follow those rules if they believe that God Himself wrote them," the high priest declares. All agree, and they proceed to debate what the Ten Rules should be. (Variations on this hypothetical can include a staged resurrection or a staged ascent to heaven on a horse.)

I ask whether such proof—believed to be empirically true—would shake their faith in their religion. In other words, how much, if any, of the religious faith of the students is based on the actual occurrence of the central "events" in their faith's religious narrative? Many students hate the question. They fight with the hypothetical: How can I be sure the camera is accurate or the scroll is authentic? You're sure! Maybe God doesn't want us to look back at history. Maybe He wants us to believe on the basis of faith. Okay, then, this is a good test: Do you believe on faith even if you're convinced the story is factually false, even fraudulent?

Finally, the students express their opinions. A considerable number of them—usually more than half—say their faith would be shaken or destroyed if the empirical basis for it was conclusively disproved. Even more say it would be destroyed by proof of knowing fraud—even well-intentioned "pious fraud."

It seems clear from Jefferson's reliance on human

observation, the laws of nature, and human reason that he would not regard these testing cases as difficult: they would confirm his conclusions about the mistaken or fraudulent nature of "revelations" and "miracles." Nor would these hypotheticals shake his belief in a nonintervening God of Nature. What might shake his belief would be the findings of scientists who could fill gaps in explaining the design of the world without recourse to a God. New scientific findings might have caused him, as they caused many others, to reconsider his reliance on the argument by design for God's existence. Though the test would be different for Jefferson than for some of my students, the process and outcome would be similar: If belief in God or religion is based on science and rationality, then the same science and rationality will eventually shake those beliefs in any person who truly has an open mind. Science and rationality, by their nature, are double-edged swords when it comes to God and religion, and playing with such swords can be dangerous to beliefs.

The difference between Jefferson and contemporary fundamentalists is that Jefferson, despite his own conclusion that it was "impossible" not to believe in "a Fabricator of all things from matter and motion," seemed open to the possibility that science might lead him, or others, away from belief in God—certainly a benevolent God. Contemporary fundamentalists, on the other hand, begin with a constant: God's existence (plus a whole lot of other beliefs, such as the divine authorship of the Bible). They use—misuse—science as a *prop* to try to convince others of what they already "know" to be true. If science were to fail to prove the existence of God, then they would assert that science was inadequate to the task. God's existence is the premise and the constant. Everything else is variable. I know some Jews who grasp at every new archaeological finding that lends any support, no matter how flimsy, to certain biblical accounts, and scoff at the absence of findings to support other biblical accounts, claiming that the absence of evidence is not evidence of absence. So, too, when science suggests that there may be benefits from the dietary laws of kashrut or the ritual laws of circumcision, these findings are trumpeted. But if science suggests no benefit, they quietly deny that these rules were designed to produce physical benefits. Heads I win, tails you lose!

Indeed, the foolishness of trying to prove the existence of God through the use of science, especially for a Christian, is evidenced by a clear contradiction between that project and the traditional Christian view of reward and punishment in the afterlife. The Christian view traditionally offers hope of salvation only to those who end up believing in God (not to mention an assortment of other supernatural phenomena). But if belief in God is to be based on empirical observation, it would be entirely irrational to attach any moral opprobrium to reaching an "erroneous" scientific conclusion based on an honest search for truth. Traditional Christians cannot have it both ways: they must either give up on claiming that belief in God is based on science; or they must give up on claiming that God will punish you for not believing in Him. Jefferson gave up on the latter.

The other important difference between Jefferson and today's fundamentalists of all religious persuasions is that

Jefferson distinguished between the existence of God, which he accepted, and the miracles of the Bible, which he rejected. For Jefferson, the latter did not follow from the former, as it does—so illogically—for many fundamentalists. Jefferson, as I pointed out, believed that "miracles"—purported deviations from Laws of Nature—were inconsistent with the God of Nature who created the rules of Nature and would not deviate from them, as he believed that the imperfect and often unjust laws of the Bible would be inconsistent with a benevolent and just God.

There is, of course, no rational relationship between the existence of a God and his purported authorship or inspiration of any particular book, whether it be the Old or New Testaments, the Koran, the Book of Mormon, or any other "sacred" script. Even if God does exist—whether He is a passive watchmaker, an active intervener, or something else—it simply does not follow that He wrote or inspired any of these books, spoke to any of the alleged prophets, or performed any of the miracles reported in these books. To be sure, if there is no God, it would follow that these books, conversations, and miracles are human contrivances, but it would not follow from the existence of God that they were not.

The essence of deism was a strong belief, based on design, in the existence of a God of Nature, and an even stronger belief that this God bears absolutely no relationship to, or responsibility for, the very flawed books and unjust actions attributed to him, or the historically corrupt churches that claim to be doing his bidding. The logical fallacy engaged in by those who would leap from the mention of God in the Declaration to the conclusion that this document was intended to accept the Judeo-Christian biblical narrative lies in their failure to understand the God-Bible non sequitur. The historical error lies in their refusal to acknowledge that the deists who drafted the Declaration believed in the nonintervening God of Nature who created the world but did not write the Bible, father Jesus, or have anything to do with Christianity, Judaism, or any other organized religion or church. Since deism—at least in name—is no longer a popular religious position, it is easier to make the mistake of associating belief in God with belief in the Judeo-Christian, or some other, organized religious dogma.

Jefferson's Views Regarding Religion in the Public Square

Jefferson was categorically opposed to public profession of religious beliefs by public figures or government officials. Indeed, according to his biographer Dumas Malone, Jefferson "made no effort to clarify his own position or make his personal religious opinions known [because] he regarded this as a wholly private matter which was nobody's business but his." As he wrote to the son of a close friend: "Religion [is] a subject on which I have ever been most scrupulously reserved. I have considered it as a matter between every man and his maker in which no other, and far less the public has a right to intermeddle."

In selecting portions of Jesus' teachings that he admired and believed in, Jefferson included the following:

and when thou prayest, thou shalt not be as the hypocrites are: for they love to pray standing in the synagogues and in the corners of the streets, that they may be seen of men . . . but thou, when thou prayest, enter into thy closet, and when thou hast shut thy door, pray to thy Father which is in secret . . . but when ye pray use not then repetitions as the heathen do: for they think they shall be heard for their much speaking.

It is not surprising therefore, that Jefferson said, "I am moreover adverse to the communication of my religious tenets to the public." He urged public figures to refuse to answer "questions of faith, which the laws have left between God and [themselves]." And as president he refused "to proclaim a national Thanksgiving Day in order not to influence religious practices of the country's people." There are some, like Akhil Reed Amar and Stephen Carter, who argue that Jefferson was opposed only to the establishment of religion by the federal government, leaving it to each state to decide whether to have an established church, but this is incorrect. He fought to disestablish the Anglican Church in Virginia on principles that were universally applicable, and "was thrilled in 1818 when the Presbyterian Church was removed as Connecticut's established church." Indeed, his entire philosophy opposed the intermingling of politics with religion at any level of government. He expressed "opposition to any form of civil religious observances." It is clear from these, and other similar statements throughout Jefferson's correspondence, that he would be deeply offended by modern politicians who wear their religion on their sleeves and who compete to outdo other politicians in their public proclamations of devotion to their religious faith. These are indeed the "hypocrites" who want their devotion to be "seen of men"—especially voters.

Those who cite the Declaration of Independence as proof that Jefferson believed in public avowals of religion should be reminded that to Jefferson, as Willard Sterne Randall put it, "religion was a private matter, like marriage, and in 1776 he said little about his private views on the subject. He did not attend church frequently, eschewed religious dogma, and believed in a supreme being who had set the world on its foundation and stepped aside." He viewed the clergy of all organized religion as corrupt, fraudulent, and dishonest—accusing them of promoting false religions. He rejected any reliance on the Bible by judges and rejected the notion—then quite prevalent—that Christianity or the Bible were part of the common law. As previously noted, he characterized such reliance as judicial "usurpation" and railed against the incorporation into English law of "laws made for the Jews alone, and the precepts of the [Christian] gospel" (much of which he characterized as "a dunghill"). He opposed "reading of the Bible by schoolchildren," and there can be little doubt that he would have opposed the posting of the Ten Commandments in public schools, especially those that commanded the worship of a particular God in a particular way and threatened punishment of children for the sins of their fathers. Indeed even today, almost nobody proposes that the full "Ten Commandments" actually be posted in schools or courthouses. What they want posted are the "Ten Bumper Stickers" or "Cliff's Notes"—abbreviated renditions of the actual commandments, since the full text contains reference to slavery, intergenerational punishment, and conflicting reasons for observing a day of rest on Saturday, not Sunday. Even this, though, would have been anathema to Jefferson's secularist views on both education and civil life.

Jefferson regarded his second-greatest contribution to the world—the first being his authorship of the Declaration of Independence—to be his work on the Virginia Statute on Religious Freedom, which, in his words, "produced the first legislature who had the courage to declare that the reason of man may be trusted with the formation of his own opinion," thereby freeing the human from the "vassalage" in which it has been held for "so many ages" by "kings, priests and nobles." He railed against laws that imposed religious tests of any kind, characterizing them as part of our long history of "religious slavery." He included atheists as within the protection of religious liberty. His third-greatest contribution was the establishment of a secular university that would, according to the authors of *The Godless Constitution*, Isaac Kramnick and R. Laurence Moore, "preserve the wall of separation intact. It would be America's first truly secular university, having no religious instruction, other than as a branch of ethics, and no professor of divinity." It may be difficult for the contemporary mind, so accustomed to today's secular university, to grasp the revolutionary nature of Jefferson's secular university at the time it was proposed. All higher education in eighteenth-century America was completely under the domination of clerics, and Jefferson's radical proposal was widely condemned by the clergy. Even as late as 1900, the president of Trinity College, subsequently renamed Duke University, urged Southerners not to send their children to colleges that were not church-sponsored. He characterized Jefferson's university as a marriage of "civil authority and infidelity" and "a deistic daring of enormous proportions." He called Jefferson "an infidel, agnostic and a materialist."

More recently, the Reverend Jerry Falwell, in urging a "return" to the good old days, ignored Jefferson's secular school but was otherwise generally accurate in his description (though wrongheaded in his prescription):

> I hope to see the day when *as in the early days of our country,* we won't have any public schools. The churches will have taken them over again and Christians will be running them. . . . We must never allow our children to forget that this is a Christian nation. We must take back what is rightfully ours.

That is, of course, precisely what Jefferson was fighting against.

No one would be more surprised than Thomas Jefferson—except perhaps his contemporaneous detractors—at how he is being portrayed by today's right-wing orthodox Christians. They have the chutzpah to claim him as the champion of *their* God, *their* Bible, *their* Christianity, and *their* desire to break down the wall of separation between church and state. Jefferson would be stunned to see the

Declaration itself being cited in support of public declarations of belief in the Judeo-Christian God. In his own time, Jefferson was seen, quite correctly, as a champion of the Enlightenment, as a critic of organized religion and a disbeliever in the divine authorship of the Bible and the theological doctrines of Christianity. Indeed, Charles B. Sanford, the author of *The Religious Life of Thomas Jefferson*, underlined that point in 1984—before recent efforts by the Religious Right to lay claim to the Declaration of Independence as a Judeo-Christian document: "Over the years since Jefferson's death those who have favored official religious observances by governmental bodies and the public schools, as well as governmental aid to religious organizations, have often perceived Thomas Jefferson as the one most responsible for America's deplorable lack of religion." They may be correct in crediting Jefferson with opposing governmental involvement in religion, but they are wrong in blaming him for America's purported "lack of religion." It is the wall of separation between church and state, so strongly supported by Jefferson, that is largely responsible for religion thriving in this country, as compared to those European countries in which church and state have been united, resulting in opposition to the church by those who disapprove of the government.

What Would Jefferson Think of Today's Religious Right?

It is always dangerous to speculate what any past historical figure would think about current issues, but in this case it seems beyond dispute that Jefferson would seek to uphold a high wall of separation between religion and government, church and state, "garden" and "wilderness." This metaphor of a "wall of separation between Church and State" derives from a letter Jefferson, as president, wrote to the Danbury Baptist Association in 1802, explaining why, as president, he would not proclaim a national fast day. In that letter he emphasized his firm belief that religion "is a matter which lies solely between man and his God" and that the powers of government do not extend to "opinions." These were not transient notions—they were central to Jefferson's religious *and* political philosophy throughout his life. As a young lawyer, his most important case involved separation of church and state. He appended to his brief in that case "a disquitation" on why the doctrines of Christianity in particular and the Bible in general are not part of the common law. He wrote:

> In truth, the alliance between church and state in England, has ever made their judges accomplice in the frauds of clergy; and even bolder than they are; for instead of being contented with the surreptitious introduction of these four chapters of Exodus, they have taken the whole leap, and declared at once that the whole Bible and Testament, in a lump, make a part of the common law of the land; the first judicial declaration which was by this Sir Matthew Hale. And thus they incorporate into the English code, laws made for the Jews alone, and the precepts of the gospel, intended by their benevolent author as

obligatory only in *foro conscientiae;* and they arm the
whole with the coercions of municipal law. They do
this, too, in a case where the question was, not at all,
whether Christianity was a part of the law of England, but simply how far the *ecclesiastical law* was to
be respected by the common law courts of England,
in the special case of a right of presentment. Thus
identifying Christianity with the ecclesiastical law of
England.

The battlefield on which the war between Enlightenment rationalism and clerical fundamentalism was fought
at the time of the Declaration of Independence was not
over the existence of God, or even the mention of God in
public declarations. Virtually every philosophical thinker in
Jefferson's time believed in some kind of God, and virtually every public document invoked God in some form.
Many even invoked Jesus. As Paine put it: "It is certain
that, in one point, all the nations of the earth and all religions agree—all believe in a God." The contentious divi-
sions were over the *nature* of God, the *methodology*
employed in deciding whether God existed, the *divinity of
the Bible,* and the *role of churches,* ministers, and priests. In
regard to *all* of these issues, Jefferson came down squarely
against traditional religion and faith, and on the side of
secular rationality. While his God was the God of Nature—
a celestial watchmaker who performed no miracles, did not
intrude into the lives of humans, and required no church
or human intermediaries—the God of traditional religion
was the God of miracles, the vengeful Jehovah, the Lord

"mighty in battle," the father of Jesus, the apex of the Christian Trinity. Jefferson's methodology rejected traditional notions of faith, revelation, and dogma in favor of science and human reason. As his letter to his nephew revealed, he did not care whether a person's reason led him to believe or disbelieve in God, as long as he backed his conclusion on reason and observation. He rejected proselytizing. He was even reticent about letting his ideas on religion influence his own family.

As his own writings demonstrate, Jefferson was convinced beyond any doubt that both the Old and New Testaments—especially the parts that describe miracles, revelations, and other supernatural phenomena—were pious frauds (he was less certain that they were pious than that they were frauds). Finally, he had no use for churches, ministers, priests, and the doctrines of organized religion. He was "anticlerical" and "rejected the moral authority of the clergy," observing that "history . . . furnishes no example of a priest-ridden people maintaining a free civil government" because "in every country and in every age, the priest has been hostile to liberty." Jefferson's "bias against institutionalized Christianity (at about the time he wrote the Declaration) extended to all Protestantism, especially Presbyterianism, as well as Catholicism and Anglicanism." He also rejected the theology of biblical Judaism, though, as Sanford explains, he expressed positive views about the Jewish people:

> The Jews excited Jefferson's sympathy because of the persecution that they had endured, especially because

they were "the parent sect and basis of Christendom." Jefferson was proud that America was the first country "to prove that religious freedom is most effectual and to restore to the Jews their social rights," he wrote to the rabbi of the Jewish synagogue in Savannah, Georgia. The United States, he wrote to John Adams, is an example to "old Europe" and is "destined to be a barrier against the return of ignorance and barbarism." He admitted to another Jewish correspondent, however, that "public opinion needs reformation [of] the prejudices still scowling on your religion."

The Declaration of Independence reflected Jefferson's thinking on these matters. By invoking "the Laws of Nature and of Nature's God" rather than the Judeo-Christian God, it made clear that it was not a Christian document, that it did not reflect uniquely Christian or Judeo-Christian beliefs, and that it was not "a bridge between the Bible and the Constitution." To the contrary, it rejected Christianity, along with other organized religions, as a basis for governance, and it built a wall—rather than a bridge—between the Bible and the Constitution.

In his final letter, on the eve of the fiftieth anniversary of the Declaration of Independence—the day on which both he and John Adams were to die—Jefferson confirmed that this historic document declared our independence not only from British political control but also from European clerical control:

May it [the Declaration of Independence] be to the world, what I believe it will be (to some parts sooner, to others later, but finally to all), the signal of arousing men to burst the chains under which monkish ignorance and superstition had persuaded them to bind themselves, and to assume the blessings and security of self-government. That form which we have substituted, restores the free right to the unbound exercise of reason and freedom of opinion. All eyes are opened, or opening, to the rights of man. The general spread of the light of science has already laid open to every view the palpable truth, that the mass of mankind has not been born with saddles on their backs, nor a favored few booted and spurred, ready to ride them legitimately, by the grace of God.

The last sentence of this letter to Roger C. Weightman was a reference to Jefferson's particular hatred of the apostle Paul, as well as of John Calvin, who preached a "predestinator God" who, in the words of Bolingbroke, "elects some of his creatures to salvation . . . and others to damnation even in the womb of their mothers." Jefferson wrote to John Adams the following:

I can never join Calvin in addressing his god. He was indeed an atheist, which I can never be; or rather his religion was one of daemonism. If ever man worshipped a false god, he did. The Being described in his 5 points, is not the God whom you and I acknowledge and adore, the Creator and benevolent Governor of the world but a daemon of malignant spirit. It would be more pardonable to believe in no god at all, than to blaspheme Him by the atrocious attributes of Calvin.

Jefferson thus intended his great document of liberty, with its "theology born of 'Nature's God,'" to attack "two claims of absolute authority—that of any government over its subject and that of any religion over the minds of men." Jefferson "saw the concepts of God and man upheld by orthodox theological circles in the colonies as antithetical to the Declaration's theological and political ideals." His own "heterodox theology"—which rejected organized religion in general and the doctrines of orthodox Christianity in particular—"is institutionalized in the Declaration as a primary truth and necessary corollary of its political theory." The Declaration's reliance on human reason and freedom of thought in place of "monkish ignorance and superstition" was indeed a radical departure from the manner by which European nations had governed, with its divine right of kings and its established hierarchical churches.

Many of those who seek to introduce the study of religion into the public schools quote Justice Lewis Powell's concurring opinion in the creationism case in which he said that he would "see no constitutional problem if schoolchildren were taught the nature of the Founding Fathers' religious beliefs and how these beliefs affected the attitudes of the times and the structure of our government." I wonder what Powell's reaction would have been if the antibiblical and anticlerical views of Jefferson and Paine were honestly and fully presented to impressionable young schoolchildren. Indeed, several years ago, in a debate with a representative of the Religious Right who advocated Bible study in elementary school, I proposed—for argument's sake—that *both* the Bible *and* Thomas Paine's *The Age of Reason* be taught together in public school, to present both sides. There was a nervous silence from my opponent. The last thing most proponents of teaching public school students "about" religion want is honest, objective *teaching;* what they want is exactly the kind of one-sided proselytizing in favor of religion that Jefferson so strongly opposed.

Why, Then, Did the Declaration Invoke God?

Why, then, did an "Enlightenment rationalist," "secular humanist," and "religious skeptic" such as Jefferson invoke God—even Nature's God—in his draft of the Declaration of Independence? To the early-twenty-first-century reader, who sees all around him disputes between those who support the invocation of God in public declarations and ceremonies and those who oppose it, the inclusion of God in the Declaration of Independence would seem to support the conclusion that Jefferson came down squarely on the side of the former. But to the late-eighteenth-century reader, who saw a very different debate between those who supported organized religion and those who rejected clericalism in favor of free thinking and human reason, Jefferson came down unamibiguously on the side of the latter. The Declaration of Independence was a resounding defeat for organized religion in general and traditional Christianity in particular. Indeed, the Declaration, and the godless Constitution as well, were subsequently criticized by influential clergymen who complained of their failure to acknowledge the Christian nature of the United States.

Another challenging question is how Jefferson persuaded his colleagues—first, those on the committee appointed to draft the Declaration, and second, those in the Congress who eventually approved it—to accept his un-Christian and anticlerical reference to "Nature's God" and "Creator" in place of the more orthodox reference to "Almighty God," "Jesus," or even simply "God."

The "Jesus" part of the question is simple. Despite the repeated claims over the years that the United States was founded as a Christian nation, the evidence is clear that the opposite is true. Jefferson strongly opposed "a [proposed] reference to Christ in the Virginia Act Establishing Religious Freedom." Shortly after the issuance of the Declaration and the adoption of the Constitution and the Bill of Rights, President John Adams—who was on the drafting committee of the Declaration—signed a treaty with the Barbary pirates of Tripoli, which was ratified by the Senate. That treaty, which is the best contemporaneous evidence, expressly declares that "the government of the United States is not in any sense founded on the Christian religion." This disclaimer followed the view expressed by Roger Williams—the religious leader most responsible for separating church from state in colonial America—more than a century earlier: "No civil state or country can be truly called Christian, although the Christians be in it." It would have been unthinkable for a Declaration drafted by Jefferson, with the approval of Adams and Franklin, to have invoked Jesus or Christianity. Indeed, the word "Christian" appeared only once in Jefferson's original draft: he referred derisively to King George as "the Christian king of Great Britain" who was responsible for the "execrable commerce" in slaves. This entire paragraph was stricken by the Congress.

As to the question of how the deistic, un-Christian reference to Nature's God could have gotten the approval of the drafting committee, it must be recalled that a *majority* of the five-man committee were deists and/or Unitarians—as were many leading colonialists at that time. In fact, Leo Pfeffer lists George Washington, Patrick Henry, George Mason, James Madison, Benjamin Franklin, Thomas Paine, John Adams, and, of course, Thomas Jefferson among the most prominent leaders of the time who were influenced by deism or Unitarianism. Three of those leaders were on the drafting committee, which consisted of Jefferson, John Adams, Benjamin Franklin, Roger Sherman, and Robert R. Livingston.

Franklin described himself as "a thorough deist" and "reject[ed] his Christian upbringing." He also was a Freemason who subscribed to the notion of God as "the Great Architect." He supported the ideas of Thomas Paine and "never came to accept the Bible as the divine revelation or Jesus as the son of God." Although he "seldom attended any public worship," he believed in a divinity—probably the same "clockmaker" God of Nature in whom Jefferson believed. "At one point he expressed a belief in a single supreme God who supervised a number of lesser gods, one of whom created our world," and he "ridiculed the idea that either Adam's sin or the righteousness of Christ could be inherited or 'imputed' to Adam's posterity." There does not appear to be any inconsistency between Franklin's deistic religious beliefs and those reflected in the Declaration.

John Adams, too, questioned traditional religious views throughout his life. As a young man he sided with a controversial Congregationalist minister in his hometown of Braintree, Massachusetts, who rejected Calvinist teachings and preached that the "aim of God was to advance happiness in man." His views were, according to Peter Rinaldo's *Atheists, Agnostics, and Deists in America,* "similar to [those] of the deists in that both believed in the power of reason to establish religious beliefs." Adams's father was dismayed at his son's decision to support such "unorthodox religious views." Adams's legal mentor was a brilliant and prominent local lawyer who believed that "the apostles were nothing more than a company of enthusiasts" who falsely claimed that they performed miracles, and whose word would be thrown out by any court of law. Adams was apparently influenced by these heterodox views. As he later wrote to a friend:

> The Priesthood have in all ancient nations, nearly monopolized learning. . . . And, even since the Reformation, when or where has existed a Protestant or dis-

senting sect who would tolerate a FREE INQUIRY? The blackest billingsgate, the most ungentlemanly insouciance, the most yahooish brutality is patiently endured, countenanced, propagated and applauded. But touch a solemn truth in collision with the dogma of a sect, though capable of the clearest truth, and you will soon find you have disturbed a nest, and the hornets will swarm about legs and hands and fly into your face and eyes.

In the words of the Adams biographer David McCullough, Adams was repelled by the "spirit of dogmatism and bigotry" he saw in "clergy and laity" alike, just as he was inspired by God's natural wonders and His gift to humans of "reason, to find out the truth." Like Jefferson, he saw "our nobler powers of intelligence and reason" as "the real design and true end of our existence."

Adams agreed with Jefferson in rejecting the doctrine of the Trinity and accepting the "God of nature." He wrote the following to Jefferson in 1815:

The question before the human race is whether the God of nature shall govern the world by His own laws, or whether priests and kings shall rule it by fictitious miracles? Or, in other words, whether authority is originally in the people? Or whether it has descended for 1800 years in a succession of popes and bishops, or brought down from heaven by the Holy Ghost in the form of a dove in a phial of holy oil.

Adams was critical of traditional Christianity, but he was downright bigoted toward Catholicism. His letters to Jefferson included the following:

> I do not like the reappearance of the Jesuits. . . . Shall we not have regular swarms of them here, in as many disguises as only a king of the gypsies can assume, dressed as printers, publishers, writers and school-masters? If ever there was a body of men who merited damnation on earth and in Hell, it is this society of Loyola's. Nevertheless, we are compelled by our system of religious toleration to offer them an asylum.

He characterized Catholicism as "fraudulent" and having inflicted "a mortal wound" on Christianity. Finally he asked Jefferson, rhetorically: "Can a free government possibly exist with the Roman Catholic religion?"

Jefferson may not have been correct in predicting that "there is not a young man now living in the United States who will not die an Unitarian," but apparently he was right about John Adams, who, along with his wife, Abigail, and their son, John Quincy, is buried in a crypt beneath a Unitarian church in Quincy, Massachusetts.

Although John Adams's religious views and practices were somewhat closer to conventional Christianity than Jefferson's and Franklin's, there is no inconsistency between what Adams apparently believed in 1776 and his approval of the deistic language of the Declaration of Independence. Nor can it be argued that Adams was unaware of Jefferson's un-Christian views when Adams approved the language of the Declaration. At about the time the Declaration was written, Adams had chastised Jefferson for "cast[ing] aspersions on Christianity" during a debate over a proposed day of fasting. Adams was reminded of his actions in a subsequent letter from Benjamin Rush:

> You rose and defended the motion, and in reply to Mr. Jefferson's objections to Christianity you said you were sorry to hear such sentiments from a gentleman whom you so highly respected and with whom you agreed upon so many subjects, and that it was the only instance you had ever known of a man of sound sense and real genius that was an enemy to Christianity. You suspected, you told me, that you had offended him, but that he soon convinced you to the contrary by crossing the room and taking a seat in the chair next to you.

Adams knew exactly what he was doing when he signed on to Jefferson's deistic language in the Declaration of Independence.

The religious views of Sherman and Livingston are less well known, though it seems likely that the former was a traditional Christian, while the latter was closer to Jefferson and had expressed religious views that have been characterized as "daring to the point of impiety." In any event, only Jefferson, Franklin, and Adams—among the drafting committee—had any real input into the Declaration's language before it went to the Continental Congress for ratification. The Congress did make several important changes, but it did not tamper with Jefferson's deistic formulation of "Nature's God" and a watchmaking "Creator."

Scholars agree that the debates in Congress over the Declaration are unrecoverable. The transcripts of the Continental Congress recorded neither the debates nor the amendments that were proposed. Only the changes finally adopted give us any evidence of what Congress may have thought of the Declaration as Jefferson submitted it on July 2. Carl Becker states that "since Congress sat, for these debates as a committee of the whole, the Journals give no account of either the debates or the amendments . . . only the form of the Declaration as finally adopted." As the historian Pauline Maier describes it:

> Once again the curtain fell, concealing the delegates as they moved through the document, making changes as they went along, leaving no official record of their proceedings beyond its fruit—the Declaration that, reconstituted as the Continental Congress, they finally adopted. Even the private correspondence of delegates is remarkably silent on what the Committee of the Whole did and why. Only Jefferson's notes on Congress's proceedings discuss the subject in any detail, and Jefferson was anything but a dispassionate observer as the Committee of the Whole rewrote or chopped off large sections of his draft, eliminating in the end fully a quarter of his text."

In any event, the words of the Declaration were not intended to reflect the ideas of its primary draftsman alone, or even of those members of the Continental Congress who revised and then signed the Declaration. According to the primary craftsman, it was meant to be an "expression of the American mind, and to give that expression the proper tone and spirit called for by the occasion." The "American mind" of the time was willing to accept Jefferson's deistic formulation of the source of rights as a common denominator reflecting the diverse and often heterodox religious views of those who supported independence.

"Nature's God" was a God acceptable to the deists. So, too, was the "Creator" who endowed human beings with "unalienable Rights." Jefferson believed that his watchmaker God had "impressed on the sense of every man" an instinct for certain rights. This is what he wrote to a friend in 1817 about one particular right:

My opinion on the right of Expatriation has been, so long ago as the year 1776, consigned to record in the act of the Virginia code, drawn by myself, recognizing the right expressly, and prescribing the mode of exercising it. The evidence of this natural right, like that of our right to life, liberty, the use of our faculties, the pursuit of happiness, is not left to the feeble and sophistical investigations of reason, but is impressed on the sense of every man. We do not claim these under the charters of kings or legislators, but under the King of kings. If he has made it a law *in* the nature of man to pursue his own happiness, he has left him free in the choice of place as well as mode. [Emphasis added.]

The Declaration's reference to the "Supreme Judge of the World," though added by the Congress to the original draft, also was consistent with Jefferson's deistic views of an un-Christian afterlife. He "saw the importance of a belief in eternal judgment for encouraging a moral life of service to society." Jefferson's "Judge," unlike the Christian God, did not reward or punish based on beliefs or acceptance of Jesus. Nor was the afterlife determined by predestination or election. "What really aroused Jefferson's ire was the suggestion that God judged people in the afterlife by their correct belief rather than by their behavior." By agreeing to appeal to the "Supreme Judge of the World," Jefferson was not seeking God's intervention in battle but rather his approval for the good deed of establishing independence.

Finally, the words "Divine Providence," which also were added by Congress, were not inconsistent with Jefferson's nonintervening watchmaker God. In a letter to Benjamin Rush, he wrote about the relationship between Providence and "the order of things": "When great evils happen, I am in the habit of looking out for what good may arise from them as consolations to us, and Providence has in fact so established the order of things, as that most evils are the means of producing some good."

A distinguished student of church-state relations in America, Leo Pfeffer has argued that the framers' references to God in the Declaration of Independence should not be misunderstood to suggest that the framers anticipated—or were willing to accept—that these references be taken to justify practices being championed by the Religious Right today:

It is reasonable to assume that many of the original framers of the document would have opposed the references [to God] if they had anticipated the use to which it was later put. For example, Justice [David J.] Brewer, in *Church of Holy Trinity* v. *United States,* cited the reference to Providence in the Declaration of Independence as one of the items in his long list of religious references and practice to support his conclusion that "this is a *Christian* nation." In view of Jefferson's strong opposition to the maxim that "Christianity is part of the common law," and to a reference to Christ in the Virginia Act Establishing Religious Freedom, it is quite unlikely that he would have approved this use by Justice Brewer of the reference to Providence in the Declaration of Independence.

The un-Christian Declaration of Independence was followed eleven years later by what Isaac Kramnick and R. Lawrence Moore have aptly called "the godless Constitution," in which God is never invoked and religion is mentioned but once, in the provision that "no religious test shall ever be required as a qualification to any office or public trust under the United States." Yet the parochial partisans of the Religious Right who deliberately misread history in an effort to turn the Declaration into a Christian document do the same with the Constitution. As the founder of the Religious Right's Rutherford Institute said: "The entire Constitution was written to promote a Christian order." Pat Robertson, Ralph Reed, James Dobson, and others have echoed this ahistoric fallacy.

The truth, according to the historians Kramnick and Moore, is that "Americans, in the era of the Revolution, were a distinctly unchurched people. The highest estimates for the late eighteenth century make only about 10 to 15 percent of the population church members." As Hector St. John de Crevecoeur reported: "Religious indifference is imperceptibly disseminated from one end of the continent to the other." According to historians of that era, "churches would have been almost completely empty had it not been for women." And considering the low status of women in those days, particularly with regard to politics, from which they were virtually excluded, it is fair to conclude that the churches did not have much of an impact on the Declaration, the Constitution, or other important political documents or actions of that period.

This is not to say that Americans were atheists, irreligious, or godless. "In a general way most of them were Christians," according to Kramnick and Moore, but "Americans in 1776 had a long way to go before making themselves strongly Christian or strongly anything else relating to a religious persuasion." As Carl Becker observed, the "natural order" and non-Christian deistic theologies reflected in Jefferson's draft of the Declaration "were the accepted premises, the preconceptions of most eighteenth-century thinkers, not only in America, but also in England and France." Even Alexis de Tocqueville, who is frequently quoted by the Religious Right to prove that nineteenth-century Americans were quite religious, argued that religion should not—and in America did not—involve itself in political parties or political controversies. Americans then, in truth, were far less traditionally religious, far less likely to belong to churches, and far, far less influenced in their politics by religious leaders than they are today.

Conclusion

What, then, can be fairly concluded from this history? Despite its references to "Nature's God," "Creator," "Supreme Judge," and "Divine Providence," the Declaration of Independence was a document designed to "burst the chains" with which organized religion—especially orthodox Christianity—had shackled previous governments. It was an anticlerical document that elevated nature, science, and human reason over "monkish ignorance and superstition." It represented a defeat for churches, clergymen, and faith, and a victory for "the rights of man," for the separation of church from state, and for reason. It marked the beginning of the end of the religious state and the emergence of the secular state based on the consent of the governed, rather than the revealed word of God. If they had been alive at the time, Falwell, Robertson, Dobson, and Keyes would surely have opposed it and joined with those who subsequently tried, and failed, to declare America to be a Christian nation ruled by "the Lord Jesus Christ."

According to Leo Pfeffer, attempts to constitutionalize or legislate the Christian God into our legal system have persisted throughout our history:

> Omission of reference to God or Christ in the Constitution was bitterly criticized by some during the

debates in the states during its ratification. Indeed, two Presbyterian church groups resolved not to vote at elections until the Constitution should be amended to acknowledge the sovereignty of God and Christ. Others decided on more practical measures. In 1863 representatives from eleven Protestant denominations organized the National Reform Association, one of whose principal purposes was: "to secure such an amendment to the Constitution of the United States as will declare the nation's allegiance to Jesus Christ and its acceptance of the moral laws of the Christian religion, and so indicate that this is a Christian nation, and place all the Christian laws, institutions, and usages of our government on an undeniably legal basis in the fundamental law of the land." Accordingly the next year the Association formally petitioned Congress to amend the preamble of the Constitution as to read "We, the People of the United States, *humbly acknowledging Almighty God as the source of all authority and power in the civil government, the Lord Jesus Christ as the Ruler among the nations, His revealed will as the supreme law of the land, in order to constitute a Christian government,* and in order to form a more perfect Union, establish justice, insure domestic Tranquility, provide for the common defence, promote the general Welfare, *and secure the inalienable rights and the blessings of life, liberty, and the pursuit of happiness to ourselves, our posterity, and all the people,* do ordain and establish this Constitution for the United States of America. . . ." As late as February 1951, Senator Ralph

Flanders of Vermont introduced a proposal to amend the Constitution to add an article reading:

Section 1. This nation devoutly recognizes the authority and law of Jesus Christ, Saviour and Ruler of nations through whom are bestowed the blessings of Almighty God.

Every such effort has failed. Yet those who today seek to Christianize America now—falsely—claim that the Declaration supports their very un-Jeffersonian vision of a Christian America based on the divinity of Jesus and the authority of the Bible. The language of the Declaration was as unbiblical and un-Christian as could achieve the level of consensus required to serve its purposes—close to the theology that got Spinoza excommunicated from Judaism. It distorts the historical record and insults the memory of those who drafted the Declaration to believe that Jefferson, Franklin, and Adams would have anything in common with today's evangelical Christian fundamentalists who invoke their names while rejecting the findings of science—including those of Darwin and Einstein—because they appear to conflict with a literal reading of the Bible. Jefferson, Franklin, and Adams would be turning in their graves if they knew how their views were being misused by today's Religious Right.

It is important that today's secularists not engage in a mirror-image distortion of what the Religious Right is now seeking to do. It would be wrong to conclude that the Declaration of Independence supports the entire agenda of those who would remove all references to God from public pronouncements. Although that would be my own strong personal preference, I cannot find support for it in the history or text of the Declaration. The Declaration was drafted at a different time in our history, when our population was far more homogeneous—especially with regard to religion. Almost everyone in the Colonies was a Protestant of some sort, at least nominally, and believed in some kind of God. The contentious issues of the day were different from those of our own. Whether generic references to "God" might be deemed offensive to some atheists, agnostics, separationists, or adherents to nontheistic religions was not a pressing issue. It is impossible to know for certain what its drafters and ratifiers would say about all of today's diverse church-state issues if they were living in today's very different world. Contentious special pleaders can find snippets of writings that can be cited in support of, and in opposition to, the agendas of each side, especially in the numerous letters written over so long a period by the likes of Jefferson, Adams, and Franklin. What can be said, with some degree of confidence, on the basis of a fair reading of the relevant record, is that the Declaration's primary drafters—though they believed in God—would not be on the side of those who would govern by religious authority and biblical revelation rather than by principles of democracy and reason.

To dramatize this point, I have gathered various questions sent to candidates by groups representative of the current Religious Right. These questions are designed to determine whether these candidates, who seek the endorsement of the Religious Right, pass various "litmus

tests." Those who respond—and some who do not—
are given scores and these scores are then released to the
public. It will be revealing to see how Thomas Jefferson
would have scored on these tests. As I have previously
noted, it is impossible to know for certain how eighteenth-
or nineteenth-century politicians would answer every question about current issues, but we can be very close to certain on those issues about which Jefferson felt strongly and
left a substantial written record.

Virtually every litmus test asks about religious practices
in public schools. We know that Jefferson was adamantly
opposed to teaching the Bible to schoolchildren and to
public prayers in schools.

The test also asks about the teaching of evolution and
creationism. We can be relatively certain how Jefferson
would have responded to these issues if he were alive today,
based on what I have shown he believed. He thought that
the biblical story of creation was an ignorant human con-
trivance, and although he lived before Darwin, he corresponded extensively with scientists about fossils, extinction,
and other issues of paleontology. His beliefs were based on
the findings of science, not the revelations in the Bible. He
surely would have favored the teaching of scientific evolution, not biblical creationism. But what about "scientific"
creationism that purports to rely not on biblical accounts
but rather on the findings of science? Here we can be less
certain. In one respect, Jefferson can be characterized as a
nonbiblical, scientific creationist. He believed that the God
of Nature had created human beings (as well as the rules of
human and physical nature). This belief was based on his

understanding of science. The difference between Jefferson and most contemporary religious creationists is that Jefferson was willing to be proved wrong by science, whereas most of today's creationists generally use—misuse—science to confirm what they already "know" to be true, because the Bible says so. If Jefferson was convinced, as the deeply religious Professor Stephen Carter is, that creationism is "bad science," he would reject it, as Carter does. But in Jefferson's day, proof of God's creation "by design" seemed like good science, and Jefferson accepted it. I doubt that he would accept it today.

Another question is about the governmental funding of religious schools. Jefferson was adamantly opposed to the government compelling anyone, through taxation, to support religion, even one's own religion. He called it "sinful and tyrannical" to require "a man to furnish contributions of money for the propagation of opinions which he disbelieves," and wrong to force him even to support "this or that teacher of his own religious persuasion," unless he chose to make a contribution. Jefferson would almost certainly oppose current efforts to divert taxpayer money to religious schools.

Yet another question asks whether the candidate would, if elected president, place a Nativity scene on the lawn of the White House. Jefferson, who did not believe in the virgin birth or any of the other alleged miracles surrounding the birth of the very human Jesus, would not have approved of crèches, but even if he did, he would be opposed to governmental displays of peculiarly Christian symbols.

Another common question revolves around the invocation of God on coins, in the Pledge of Allegiance, and in other ceremonial settings. Jefferson himself invoked God in the Declaration and even in his bill for establishing religious freedom in Virginia. But so did Thomas Paine and other more radical anti-Christians. Invoking God was simply not controversial in Jefferson's day, because to Jefferson it meant "Nature's God," not the Bible's God. It is impossible to know what Jefferson would think today, when invoking God is quite controversial and divisive, because it tends to mean the Judeo-Christian God of the Bible. To lean over backward, I will say that Jefferson might have received a positive score from the Religious Right on this question.

He probably would not have been in favor of abolishing, as the Religious right is, the Department of Education, the National Endowment for the Arts and Humanities, or the Office of Surgeon General, since he was so supportive of education, science, medicine, philosophy, and the arts, though he was wary of federal involvement in matters left, by the Constitution, to the states.

Other questions deal with abortion, homosexuality, pornography, assisted suicide, and stem cell research to cure diseases. There are simply insufficient data to know what Jefferson would say about abortion. He appeared to favor the criminalization of homosexuality. His views on free speech probably would have placed him on the side of those who oppose governmental censorship, even of pornography, though that is not certain. He was sympathetic to suicide. And he believed in the progress of science to cure illness.

All in all, it is fair to conclude that Thomas Jefferson

would have scored quite low—certainly less than 25 per-cent—on any Religious Right litmus test. He probably would have scored somewhere between Barney Frank and Bill Clinton. Jefferson surely would not have received the endorsement of the Religious Right for president based on his answers to their litmus test questions. Yet they now fraudulently claim his posthumous endorsement for their efforts to tear down the wall of separation between church and state, which was among his most enduring contributions to American constitutional theory and practice.

The out-of-context quotation of Jefferson that appears on his memorial in Washington, when placed back into its proper context, perhaps best summarizes Jefferson's views regarding God, on the one hand, and organized religion, on the other. The quote on the memorial invokes God: "I have sworn upon the altar of God, eternal hostility against every form of tyranny over the mind of man."

These words were selected in 1943, according to Kramnick and Moore, to convey America's "enduring commitment, as a religious people, to oppose vigilantly political oppression and tyranny in all forms—be it that of George III, German Kaisers, Hitler or Japanese aggressors." But when Jefferson wrote these words, in 1800, in the midst of his campaign for president, he directed them at the tyranny of the *clergy*. Benjamin Rush, a close friend and fellow religious skeptic, had written to Jefferson that the clergy were attacking him with claims that his election would undermine their preeminent position in American life. Jefferson's reply reads in relevant part as follows:

I promised you a letter on Christianity, which I have not forgotten. On the contrary, it is because I have reflected on it, that I find much more time necessary for it than I can at present dispose of. I have a view of the subject which ought to displease neither the rational Christian nor Deists, and would reconcile many to a character they have too hastily rejected. I do not know that it would reconcile the *genus irritable vatum* [the irritable tribe of priests] who are all in arms against me. Their hostility is on too interesting ground to be softened. . . . The successful experiment made under the prevalence of that delusion on the clause of the Constitution, which, while it secured the freedom of the press, covered also the freedom of religion, had given to the clergy a very favorite hope of obtaining an establishment of a particular form of Christianity through the United States; and as every sect believes its own form the true one, every one perhaps hoped for his own, but especially the Episcopalians and Congregationalists. The returning good sense of our country threatens abortion to their hopes, and they believe that any portion of power confided to me, will be exerted in opposition to their schemes. And they believe rightly: for I have sworn upon the altar of God, eternal hostility against every form of tyranny over the mind of man. But this is all they have to fear from me; and enough too in their opinion.

The man who drafted the Declaration of Independence was a man willing to invoke his God—the God of Nature—against organized churches and irritable clerics who would impose "tyranny over the mind of man" by establishing their religious doctrines—or any religious doctrine—as the only truth. As Kramnick and Moore summarized it: "Jefferson was not a godless man or intrinsically irreligious. While committed to the strict separation of church and state, to a godless politics, and thus fiercely anticlerical, he was also a man of deeply felt *private* religious conviction."

It is this distinction between *private beliefs* and *public politics*—a distinction central to Jefferson and many of his contemporaries—that is ignored, even distorted, by today's public panderers of the Religious Right, who miscite the Declaration in support of their parochial causes—to borrow an apt phrase from Carl Becker—"without fear and without research."

2

What Are "the Laws of Nature and of Nature's God"?

Why "Natural Law" Was Invoked

According to the Declaration of Independence, the right of the colonists to separate from Great Britain was based on "the Laws of Nature and of Nature's God." This resort to "natural law" raises profound questions as to the source, basis, and "unalienab[ility]" of this or any other "right." "Natural" law, as distinguished from "positive" legal enactments, is not necessarily found in any codified legislation or judicial decisions. It derives from divine or natural principles rather than from "the consent of the governed." When a right does emanate from "the consent of the governed"—from existing positive legal enactments such as the Constitution or the Bill of Rights—its source is more readily identifiable and its significance more easily understood.

We find comfortable justification for the moral force of this consent in the basic tenets of democratic theory, social contract, and other currently accepted values. The people themselves, the "governed," have decided to entrench, in our governing documents, certain fundamental liberties and limitations, which they designate as "rights," rather than mere preferences, and make these rights difficult to repeal, even by subsequent majorities.

Our own Constitution requires a deliberately cumbersome amending process. Though it has been invoked numerous times throughout our history, it has generally been used to expand rights (such as the right to vote), to create new rights (such as the right not to be enslaved and to equal protection of the laws), and to correct errors or anachronisms in the original document that became evident on the basis of new experiences (such as the development of the party system). No fundamental right, once created by the positive law of our Constitution, has ever been repealed. In fact, it is fair to say that most of the rights enumerated in the original Constitution and Bill of Rights have been expanded by judicial construction (a uniquely American genre of positive law) beyond their original intent.

This does not necessarily mean that such positive rights are "unalienable"—either in practice or in theory. For example, during wars and other national emergencies, many rights deemed fundamental during peacetime have been restricted, at least temporarily. Even now, following the events of September 11, 2001, we are seeing certain rights contracting before our very eyes—or even worse, deliberately hidden from our view by claims of necessary secrecy. Since the current national security emergency is not likely to end in the foreseeable future, these contractions may be long-term if not permanent. The rights that have been curtailed may not be among the most fundamental—at least for those not directly affected—but certainly they are not trivial.

The point is that rights lie along a continuum of importance, and the more fundamental they are, the more likely they are to be seen as "unalienable." Rights also lie along a continuum of generality, with "Life, Liberty, and the Pursuit of Happiness" at the most general and abstract end, and more "technical" rights, such as those announced in the *Miranda* decision, at the most specific and concrete end. The more abstract a right, the more "unalienable" (and uncontroversial) it will seem, since rights articulated at a high level of abstraction can mean all things to all people and can change in content over time and place without alienating the broad terms of the right itself.

The abstract rights articulated in the Declaration were not derived from positive—that is, enacted—law. These included the right to secede and the rights to life, liberty, and the pursuit of happiness. It would be interesting to speculate about which other rights might have been in the minds of the drafters. Perhaps the Bill of Rights, adopted ten years later, provides some clues. The rights enumerated in the Declaration, however, did not rely on any governing legislation or judicial decision. The Declaration did not invoke the "known law and statutes" of Great Britain, as the English Declaration of Rights had done in 1689. That should not be surprising, since the primary purpose of the

Declaration was to provide a justification for an extralegal action—the "treasonous" and "criminal" act of secession and separation. Indeed, had the revolution failed, its leaders would certainly have been subject to criminal prosecution. In the absence of binding international law that provided for the right of secession or self-determination, there was no positive law to which the colonists could appeal for justification of their actions.

The classic alternative to positive law has, since the time of the Greeks and then Aquinas, been "natural law." Another alternative has been "the law of necessity" (thought to be an oxymoron by some), which finds some support both in natural and positive law. The Declaration, in fact, invoked such necessity in its formulation as well. "Natural law" based on divine revelation—the source of Christian natural law for Aquinas—was anathema to Jefferson. Since there was no existing positive law that supported secession, and since Jefferson would not invoke revealed biblical law, he needed a source beyond positive law but within the realm of human reason and experience. Hence "the Laws of Nature and of Nature's God," which Jefferson and his fellow deists believed could be derived from observing the design of the universe and of human nature, as the Stoics had done centuries earlier. The right to secede, along with the rights to life, liberty, and the pursuit of happiness were, according to Jefferson, divinely revealed law, but in a very different sense than the laws of the Bible. They were, instead, revealed in the "Laws of Nature" and endowed to all human beings by "Nature's God." Moreover, it did not take a philosopher, a prophet, or a theologian to translate these laws to the average person. They were "self-evident" in the sense that they were "impressed on the sense of every man," who was equipped with an innate moral sense of right and wrong. Jefferson even thought that this moral sense was a *more* reliable way of discovering our rights than relying on abstract reason. He famously wrote, "State a moral case to a ploughman and a professor. The former will decide it as well, and often better than the latter, because he has not been led astray by artificial rules."

It was thus unimportant to Jefferson whether the American colonists could offer abstract philosophical justifications for the natural rights that led them to demand their independence, because these farmers and merchants "felt their rights before they had thought of their explanation." These rights were "law in the nature of man." God had endowed human beings with their nature—which included a moral instinct—and this nature led inexorably to natural rights. According to Jefferson, man's instinctive moral sense is "as much a part of our constitution as that of feeling, seeing or hearing." There is, as we shall see, a twofold problem with this approach to the source of rights—one logical, the other empirical. First, any approach that derives the "ought" of morality from the "is" of nature—even human nature—commits the classic "naturalistic fallacy." Second, even if moral conclusions could be drawn from nature, there is considerable doubt whether human beings are in fact born with an instinct for justice. Jefferson's observations about human nature, it turns out, may simply be untrue.

Does It Matter Whether "the Laws of Nature and of Nature's God" Exist?

In his 1922 seminal book *The Declaration of Independence,* Carl Becker argues that "to ask whether the natural rights philosophy of the Declaration of Independence is true or false is essentially a meaningless question." He is wrong. The question of whether rights actually come from nature is meaningful and important. It is and always was an empirical question, subject to proof or disproof. It contains a null hypothesis. It is either true or false as a matter of fact, and it appears to be false by Jefferson's own standards of science and reason.

In the years since Jefferson—and Carl Becker—wrote, scientists have conducted experiments designed to determine whether human beings are born with certain dispositions, instincts, or attitudes. It would be impossible, of course, to establish, as a scientific matter, whether any such "inherent" characteristics, if they were indeed "impressed on the sense of every man," come from "their Creator," in the sense of an external God, or from some other, more biological, source. But it is possible, though quite difficult, to test for whether certain characteristics are more "inborn" or "acquired"—more "nature" or "nurture." This quest has been complicated by scientific findings that the structure of the brain, particularly the connections of synapses, continues to take shape not only *in utero* but even after birth. Thus nature is influenced by nurture even in something so basic as the physiology of the brain. These findings suggest that nature and nurture are on a continuum rather than separated by a sharp distinction, but they do not remove the question from the realm of scientific inquiry. If anything, these findings make this question even more subject to the complexities and nuances of science.

Nor is there anything approaching consensus about the existence of a moral sense in the nonscientific literature. Some modern thinkers, such as the philosopher John Rawls, seem to believe that there is some "intuitionistic" predisposition toward justice. Rawls writes about "innate categories of morality common to all men imprinted in their neural structure." Others, such as the legal philosopher Ronald Dworkin, reject that notion, pointing out that even in the United States and Britain, the majority of citizens "do not exercise the political liberties that they have, and would not count the loss of these liberties as especially grievous." Such speculations, however, can hardly count as empirical, and the obvious disagreements among thinkers show that the theory of an inborn moral sense is anything but self-evident.

The bottom line is thus that Jefferson's "observations" on human nature turn out to be empirically questionable at best. No valid scientific study has ever convincingly demonstrated a "gene" for justice, an instinct for liberty, or even an inborn predisposition toward the rights of others. The various rights he mentioned in the Declaration—secession, life, liberty, and the pursuit of happiness—do not seem to be "impressed on the sense of every man." They must be learned, and many human beings around the world seem to have difficulty learning them. Far too many place little value on the lives of others; they welcome authority; and they accept lives of misery. Dostoyevsky may have been closer to the truth when he observed, through one of his characters, that human beings crave "miracle, mystery, and authority" and that "nothing has been more insupportable for a man and a human society than freedom." On the basis of Dostoyevsky's view of what is impressed on the human mind, he predicted that if people begin "to build their tower of Babel without [the authority of the church], they will end, of course, with cannibalism." This pessimistic assessment, too, may be off the mark, but it is an empirical assessment, subject to the canons of science and the null hypothesis, just as Jefferson's more optimistic assessment of human nature is capable of being proved right or wrong. And it matters greatly whether it is Jefferson or Dostoyevsky who is closer to the truth. It is anything but "essentially meaningless" to ask whether "the natural rights philosophy of the Declaration of Independence is true or false," as Becker argued, since an empirically based philosophy cannot serve as a foundation for human rights if its essential underlying factual assumptions are false.

One reason why it is important—and certainly not "essentially meaningless"—to question the empirical basis of Jefferson's natural law is that if Jefferson were correct about rights being "impressed on the sense of every man," then the need for *legally entrenched rights* would actually *diminish*. It is precisely because most people have little appreciation for rights—at least until they or their loved ones stand to benefit from them in the short term—that it is so important to build them into the structure of government, as the United States subsequently did in the Constitution and the Bill of Rights. Rights, to the extent that they are different from the mere preferences of shifting majorities, are what Ronald Dworkin calls "trumps" on legislation, referenda, and other mechanisms of majority rule. Rights rule over preferences, even strong preferences. To designate something "a right" is to give it a special status above other interests. If all people—or even a constant majority of all people—had rights permanently "impressed" on their senses, there would be less need for such countermajoritarian (and in that sense undemocratic) trumps.

The rights enumerated by Jefferson in the Declaration were majoritarian in nature—at least in the context of separation from Great Britain. A majority of "one people" (colonial Americans) were being denied these rights by "another" people (Great Britain) and their king. They were *our* rights in relation to *them*. Perhaps self-serving rights are impressed on most human beings (along with self-serving nonrights), but the rights of *others*, which may take something away from *us*, must be learned from experience to be appreciated. A longer view is necessary to understand that granting rights to others—even when they disadvantage you in the short run—may be important to the stability of a society, and thus to the benefit of all in the long run. But most human beings seem to prefer the short-term certainty of immediate gratification to the long-term probability of more ultimate satisfaction. Rights, to the extent that they exchange immediate personal gratification for more long-term social stability, seem counterinstinctive.

It should not be surprising that there was little controversy within the United States about the right to secede—that decision had already been made by the time the Declaration was ratified. The time for debate was over. This is not to suggest that the decision to secede itself was without controversy—there were many dissenters who remained to be persuaded—but even some who believed it would be imprudent to secede still believed there was a *right* to do so. There was even less controversy about the rights to life, liberty, and the pursuit of happiness, since those rights, stated abstractly, benefit everyone. The real rights controversy, as we will see in chapter 3, centered around the right of equality—if, indeed, the Declaration's expression of the "self-evident" truth "that all Men are created equal" was an assertion of a right at all. Any claim of equality benefits the less advantaged at the expense of the more advantaged. In the context of slavery, equality would come to mean—at least for abolitionists—that slaveowners could lose their valuable "property" if slaves were deemed their equals and thus not subject to their legal domination. As the Jefferson scholar Joseph J. Ellis has observed:

> In 1861, for example, Lincoln thought the words of the Declaration justified a war against slavery, while leaders of the Confederacy thought the same words justified rebellion against the tyranny of the federal government led by Lincoln.

The rights stated in the Declaration, however, are so abstract as to be nearly meaningless. If Jefferson could indeed assert them as self-evident, it was only because they are stated in so broad a manner that their controversial application to any particular problem of policy is obscured by the fog of generality. Everyone can agree on the importance of rights to life, liberty, and the pursuit of happiness, but only because agreement about such sweeping terms amounts to almost no binding agreement at all.

For example, the abstract right to life is uncontroversial, but when reduced to its particulars, it provokes the most divisive disputes. This right has been cited by opponents of abortion, capital punishment, assisted suicide, war, deadly force, animal rights, and other hot-button issues. It also has been cited by proponents of abortion (the mother's right to life), capital punishment (the rights of future victims), gun control, just war, deadly force, and medical research on animals. The right to life has become an emotional cliché equally available to all sides on every life-and-death issue.

The right to liberty has been invoked as the equivalent of John Stuart Mill's famous principle—articulated years after the Declaration—denying government the power to compel any individual to do, or refrain from doing, anything that has an impact only on the individual and not on other people. Jefferson anticipated Mill with regard to religious rights. His *An Act for Establishing Religious Freedom*—one of the three contributions for which he wanted to be remembered—included the following:

that the opinions of men are not the object of civil government, nor under its jurisdiction; that to suffer the civil magistrate to intrude his powers into the field of opinion and to restrain the profession or propagation of principles on supposition of their ill tendency is a dangerous fallacy, which at once destroys all religious liberty, because he being of course judge of that tendency will make his opinions the rule of judgment, and approve or condemn the sentiments of others only as they shall square with or differ from his own; that it is time enough for the rightful purposes of civil government for its officers to interfere when principles break out into overt acts against peace and good order.

The broad right to liberty can, of course, be invoked to justify any action. The British philosopher Jeremy Bentham believed that any law—even one prohibiting murder—is an "infraction" of liberty, but that many such infractions are justified by the greater good. So defined, the general right to liberty, as distinguished from more particular rights to specific liberties, becomes meaningless. Ronald Dworkin, in *Taking Rights Seriously,* has asked and sought to answer the question "Do we have a right to liberty?"

Thomas Jefferson thought so, and since his day the right to liberty has received more play than the competing rights he mentioned to life and the pursuit of happiness. Liberty gave its name to the most influential political movement of the last century, and many of those who now despise liberals do so on the ground that they are not sufficiently libertarian. Of course, almost everyone concedes that the right to liberty is not the only political right, and that therefore claims to freedom must be limited, for example, by restraints that protect the security or property of others. Nevertheless the consensus in favor of some right to liberty is a vast one, though it is . . . misguided.

Dworkin argues that belief in a right to liberty is misguided because equality is a more fundamental right and "laws are needed to protect equality, and laws are inevitably compromises of liberty." Thus for Dworkin "in any strong sense of right, which would be competitive with the right of equality, there exists no general right to liberty at all."

Other thinkers recognize additional claims against liberty, such as security, community, and responsibility. Under this view, liberty is what is left to the individual after other stronger or more legitimate claims have been satisfied, or at least balanced. If "Nature's God" is the God of the gaps, then liberty is the philosophy of the gaps.

The pursuit of happiness, like the right to liberty, is far too individualistic and open-ended to provide a blueprint, or even a general guide, for resolution of conflicting claims. What makes one person happy may make another miserable. H. L. Mencken once defined Puritanism as "the haunting fear that someone, somewhere may be happy." And George Bernard Shaw quipped: "Do not do unto others as they should do unto you—their tastes may be different." A general right to pursue happiness, like a general right to liberty, makes no specific policy claims—rather, it is what is left after other, competing, legitimate claims have been satisfied or balanced.

To characterize the right to secession or rights to life, liberty, and the pursuit of happiness as natural, God-given, and unalienable is to attribute to Nature and to God a prudential limitation on governmental power based on long and unhappy experiences with governments of unlimited powers—governments that also claimed to be based on the natural and divine "right" of rulers. But to make these rights seem natural or "self-evident" to people of varying natures, they must be stated in terms so abstract as to hide their sometimes controversial applications and to make them little more than clichés of comfortable consensus. As we will see, the authority to give them any *real* meaning lies with people, not with Nature or God.

Does Natural Law Exist, or Is It a Fiction?

Invoking natural law may be a useful, even sometimes effective, way of trumping other people's preferences in the absence of positive-law trumps, such as a constitution. For example, based on our current interpretation of the U.S. Constitution, a fetus has no constitutional right—or other positive-law right—not to be aborted if the mother so chooses. So antiabortion advocates invoke a natural-law "right to life" on behalf of the fetus. Some ground this natural-law right in their interpretation of divine revelation, while others ground it in their interpretation of the laws of nature. The same is true of the death penalty, which is explicitly authorized by the Constitution. Hence some opponents of capital punishment invoke the "right to life" even on behalf of convicted murderers.

Natural law, to those who believe in it, is an argument stopper—the ace of trumps. After all, if God Himself revealed the law, how can a mere mortal argue with it? Or if the law derives inexorably from Nature, how can it be wrong? As Juvenal put it: "Never does Nature say one thing and wisdom another."

Jeremy Bentham once quipped that people invoke natural law "when they wish to get their way without having to argue for it." To that I would add, "and without having to persuade a majority, or a court, to agree with them." It is right (and its opposite is wrong) just because they claim God or Nature said so. End of the discussion.

The most compelling argument for invoking natural law is that we need it. Without it we have no basis—at least no legal basis—for opposing or resisting unjust laws that have been properly enacted. British control of the colonies was legitimated by repeated acts of Parliament. It was lawful, at least according to English positive law. But Jefferson believed there were higher laws—"the Laws of Nature and of Nature's God"—that trumped English positive law, especially since the colonists were not represented in the English Parliament (as many, probably most, British subjects were not represented in those days of limited suffrage). It is not surprising that only a decade after the

Declaration invoked natural law, the Constitution seemed to eschew reliance on anything but positive law—revolutionaries need natural law to justify their extralegal actions against the positive law of their enemies, but as soon as these same revolutionaries establish a new government, they can rely on "their own" positive law.

It is one thing to say that natural law is a useful, even essential, legal fiction for a civilized world. It is quite another thing to say that it actually exists. A cure for breast cancer would be useful as well, but until and unless one actually exists, it is fraudulent and dangerous to pretend that we have it. The reality is that natural law simply does not exist, no matter how much we "need" it or wish it existed. It is a human invention, much like organized religion. And it may be beneficial or harmful, much like organized religion. But even if it is beneficial, that doesn't make it any more real than a placebo that works.

There are, after all, only three basic sources of human knowledge: discovery, invention, and devine revelation. The physical rules of nature actually exist, and await discovery by human beings. (They would, of course, exist even in the absence of human beings, as they did for billions of years. They just would not be called "rules," because there would be no one to understand or even name them.) Newton discovered some, Einstein others, and Darwin yet others. If these giants had not discovered these rules when they did, it is reasonable to assume that other geniuses, who came after them, would have made these (or similar) discoveries, since the rules are out there waiting to be discovered, much as America was out there waiting to be found by Leif Eriksson or Christopher Columbus—or some other European, Asian, or African explorer—had the earlier explorers been drowned while attempting to cross the Atlantic. (America, like the rules of Nature, was also out there before human beings, and would have remained there had it not been "discovered"—along with its native population—by Europeans.)

Inventions are different. They require the creative combining of different kinds of knowledge and information—both theoretical and practical—to design something that did not previously exist. Simple inventions, such as the cotton gin or the automobile, would have been made by others if those responsible for inventing them had never lived. Complex, more individualistic inventions, such as Beethoven's symphonies, Picasso's paintings, Shakespeare's plays, or Rube Goldberg's contraptions would never have been replicated by others, at least not exactly. They are truly unique. We call them "inspired," but they are human inventions. There are also, of course, many things that fall somewhere between discovery and invention, and there are overlaps. This is because inventions often require discoveries, and vice versa.

Finally, there is divine revelation, for those who believe in it. Like discovery and invention, revelation lies along a continuum. Some people believe that God actually spoke to particular human beings, handed them tablets, or dictated entire books. Others believe that God inspires human conduct in ways that are not subject to human understanding. Yet others, such as Jefferson and his fellow deists, believed that God created the rules of both physical and human nature, and that any human being, by observing these rules, can see God's will revealed (discovered) without the intermediation of churches, Bibles, or ministers.

Into which of these categories do laws, rights, and morality fit? Positive law is plainly a human invention. Madison's Constitution, for example, with its emphasis on division of power, checks and balances, and separation of church and state, is an experiment based on human experience—mostly negative—with other types of government. Churchill seemed to agree with this experimental approach when he characterized democracy as "the worst form of government except all those other forms that have been tried from time to time." It is an attempt to improve on the past (and on human nature). Like most human inventions, it builds on the prior inventions and discoveries of predecessors. Also like most inventions, it is imperfect and requires a process for its own change and improvement.

Natural law, on the other hand, purports to be a product of discovery and/or divine revelation. It is a fully developed and flawless entity, simply waiting to be discovered or discerned by human beings so they can live by its principles. As Jeremy Bentham once observed in a related context, this is "nonsense on stilts." It is supernatural superstition. There is simply no such thing waiting to be discovered, certainly nothing perfect and unchanging. All laws, in the sense of prescriptive rules of conduct and morality, are imperfect and ever-changing human inventions, for which we, as their inventors, are ultimately responsible. Natural law, and all of its variations, are also human inventions dressed up by humans as discoveries and divine revelations, to give them greater authority. They are, ultimately, no more than legal or moral fictions.

Is Natural Law a Necessary, or Even Useful, Fiction?

In addition to the question of whether natural law is a fiction—a human invention—there is the question of whether natural law is a beneficial or a harmful fiction. When it is invoked to produce a "good" result—to persuade individuals not to obey the "lawful" commands of evil tyrants—we all approve of it (ironically because we conclude that the end justifies the means—a very non-natural-law criterion for evaluating anything!). But we must recall that natural law also has been invoked in support of the worst of actions—including slavery, racism, sexism, and even terrorism.

At bottom, natural law is an invitation to self-righteous lawlessness (both positive and negative), in the sense that it provides a justification for refusing to obey positive law. We applaud such lawlessness when it is directed against Nazism and slavery, but often condemn it when it leads to terrorism, the blocking of abortion clinics, or the refusal to pay taxes. Natural law is a double-edged sword aimed at the heart of democracy and the rule of law, since these important mechanisms necessarily rely on a positive law equally accessible to all.

Jefferson himself used natural law and "natural rights" as an undemocratic tactic to discourage subsequent majorities from changing the good laws he wrote. In his *An Act for Establishing Religious Freedom*, Jefferson included a section containing the following admonition to future legislators:

> though we well know this Assembly elected by the people for the ordinary purposes of legislation only, have no power to restrain the acts of succeeding assemblies, constituted with the powers equal to our own, and that therefore to declare this act irrevocable would be of no effect in law; yet we are free to declare, and do declare, that the rights hereby asserted are of the natural rights of mankind, and that if any act shall be hereafter passed to repeal the present or to narrow its operation, such act will be an infringement of natural right.

Thus, instead of trying to persuade the governed to make it difficult, by positive law, to amend the right to religious liberty, Jefferson played his trump card: natural law.

Jefferson believed it was a natural right of humankind not to be compelled "to furnish contributions of money for the propagation of opinions which he disbelieves" and to "be free to profess, and by argument to maintain, their opinion in matters of religion." I certainly agree that such rights *should* be recognized—indeed, entrenched—by the law, since experience demonstrates that if they are not recognized, many evils will follow. But I do not see them in nature. Even if the opposite were "natural"—even if there were a genetic predisposition toward believing in and imposing one true religion—I would still argue for the right to religious freedom and dissent. Nor does "revealed law" support these rights. Jefferson argued that if God, who is all-powerful, wanted everyone to follow the same religion, they would. This reductionist argument would also lead to the conclusion that if God wanted a world without murder, rape, and child abuse, we would be living in that world. The fact is that many religions—Catholicism, Puritanism, and Islam among them—have long advocated mandatory contributions to propagate their faith and punishment for those who advocate a different one. (On the day I was reviewing the draft manuscript for this book, I read in the newspaper that the Catholic Church finally decided that it had been theologically improper to try to convert the Jews. Whoops! Sorry for all those inquisitions, crusades, and autos-da-fé. Previous popes were wrong—infallible, perhaps, but wrong.) Jefferson's rights are important, not because human nature supports them, but because it does *not*. The right to dissent from the consensus of religious or other views reflects unnatural law—*nurtural* law—at its best. It is the function of rights to change human nature, or at least to provide a counterpoint to human nature, based on human experience.

A striking example of how natural law can be, and was, used to produce evil results can be seen in an 1872 decision of the U.S. Supreme Court, denying women the right to practice law. In *Bradwell* v. *State of Illinois,* the lower court had invoked Jefferson's concepts of "natural law" and God as "designer" to argue that "God designed the sexes to occupy different spheres of action. It belonged to men to apply and execute the law." The role assigned by nature to women was in the "domestic sphere." A justice of the Supreme Court invoked divine law: "The paramount destiny and mission of woman are to fulfill the noble and benign office of wife and mother. This is the law of the Creator." We now recognize how downright stupid, ignoble, and malignant this divine design argument is, as applied to women by men, but even if it were somehow true that most women were "designed" by nature or told by God to stay home and darn the socks, it still would be wrong to deny a woman who wanted to challenge nature the right to try something she was not "designed" to do.

Natural law was used to justify slavery because of the "natural" differences between whites and blacks, and to support the criminalization of "unnatural" male homosexuality (which was called "the crime against nature"). What I have argued elsewhere about divine law also can be said about natural law:

> To be an advocate of divine law is to always have to say you're sorry for the mistakes of your predecessors, as your successors will inevitably have to apologize for the mistakes you are now making when you claim to know God's true intentions. It insults God to believe that it was he who mandated eternal inequality for women, execution for gays, slavery, animal sacrifice, and the scores of other immoral laws of the Bible, the Koran, and other books that purport to speak in God's name. Humans are to blame for these immoralities, just as humans must be credited with the hundreds of morally elevating laws of these holy

books. And it is humans who must continue to change law and morality so as to remain more elevated than the animals who indeed cannot rise above the law of nature and of the jungle. In a diverse world where many claim to know God's will, and where there is consensus about neither its content nor the methodology for discerning it, God should not be invoked as the source of our political rights. In any event, for the millions of good and moral people who do not believe in God, or in an intervening God—or who are agnostic about these matters—there must be other sources of morality, law, and rights.

The fundamental flaw in any attempt to derive moral conclusions from the operation of nature is the failure to recognize that nature is morally neutral. As Robert B. Ingersoll correctly observed: "In nature there are neither rewards, nor punishments; there are only consequences." Its rules existed before human consciousness, and they would have operated even if no human being ever appeared in the world. Nature does what it does because of factors entirely irrelevant to human morality. As Anatole France once put it: "Nature has no principles, she furnishes us with no reason to believe that human life is to be respected. Nature, in its indifference, makes no distinction between good and evil." Anyone who seeks to derive moral conclusions directly from descriptions of nature necessarily indulges in a variation on what has been called the "naturalistic fallacy." This classic fallacy has been described in the following terms: "The naturalistic fallacy states that it is logically impossible for any set of statements of the kind usually called descriptive to entail a statement of the kind usually called evaluative."

This is not to deny that there may be a relationship between nature and morality. Any attempt to build a system of morality that completely ignores nature will fail. Nature has a vote but not a veto on questions of morality. In deciding on a sexual morality appropriate for a given society, it is important to understand the nature of the sex drive. For example, efforts to deter adolescent masturbation as "unnatural" and therefore "wrong" are doomed to failure because the nature of adolescent sexuality is more powerful than the threats of punishment for this entirely harmless—and I would add "natural"—outlet. Many Catholics are now questioning whether priestly celibacy is incompatible with the natural sex drive. But even if sociobiologists were to prove that men are naturally inclined to force women into sexual submission, it would be morally wrong for a society not to make every reasonable effort to hold this "natural impulse" in check, because even if it is natural, it is wrong. "Doing what comes naturally" may be a good song title, but it is a terrible rule of morality. Rape is horribly wrong even though the men who wrote the Bible did not think it was wrong enough to include in the Ten Commandments while including voluntary adultery, but only if it involved a married *woman!* We can do better than the Ten Commandments because we have much more human experience on which to base our rules than did those who wrote the Bible.

Morality evolves with experience, and nature is part of that experience but not the only part. In constructing a moral code, one should not ignore the varieties of human nature, but the diverse components of nature cannot be translated directly into morality. The complex relationship between the *is* of nature and the *ought* of morality must be mediated by human experience. To ignore the complex relationships among nature, nurture, experience, and morality and to seek to derive moral conclusions directly from nature is to commit a particularly dangerous variation on the naturalistic fallacy. Patrick Buchanan misused nature when he characterized AIDS as "nature's retribution" against gay men for "violating the laws of nature," as did the ultra-Orthodox rabbi who declared the Holocaust to be God's punishment of the Jews for eating pork.

Among the most vocal indulgers in the naturalistic fallacy is Alan Keyes—former presidential candidate, national television talk show host, and prominent speaker. In a speech to impressionable public high school students at Hylton High School in Virginia, Keyes claims that to accept the scientific evidence in support of evolution—which he rejects because he does not believe that his "early relatives were monkeys"—necessarily requires belief in the immoral principle that "might makes right" and that "justice" should come "only for the strong." (This misguided claim is very different from arguing that belief in evolution will *lead* to belief in might makes right, which is an empirical claim that can be tested by science. Indeed, history seems to show that religious claims, which tend to be absolute, have been decided by might more often than by right.) He even erroneously claims that "this is what our children learn" in the public schools. I would challenge him to cite a single example of this. He also suggests that this philosophy is what leads women to choose abortion, since the mother is stronger than the fetus. He argues, therefore, that we should not "respect" or "care about" the "results" of evolution.

This kind of confused thinking, which fails to understand the basic differences between the *is* of science and the *ought* of morality, is a throwback to the Middle Ages, when the church claimed a monopoly on both morality and science and burned people for believing that the earth revolved around the sun, as promiscuously as it burned people for believing that Jesus was not the son of God. This way of thinking has been repudiated not only by contemporary science and philosophy but also by virtually all modern religious groups, including the Catholic Church, to which Keyes subscribes. The Catholic Church accepts the scientific findings of evolution but categorically rejects the despicable and immoral belief that "might makes right" or that justice is for the strong alone. Indeed, it opposes abortion as a moral matter while accepting evolution as a scientific truth—a dichotomy Keyes finds hard to accept.

Keyes also argues that without an intelligent creator—in his view, the God of the Bible—there can be no truth, even scientific truth. His non sequitur goes something like this: Truth requires "a kind of intelligent cohesion that could ultimately be known and understood." And if we have "dispensed with the idea of an intelligent creator," we can have no truth! He confuses, of course, "intelligence" as a source of nature with "intelligible" as a way of understanding nature. We are perfectly capable of understanding—that is, making intelligible—a phenomenon produced without intelligence. Scientists understand the random movement of particles, the division of single-cell organisms, the spasms of unconscious patients, and myriad other physical phenomena. Unless Keyes is relying on the tautology that every phenomenon is the product of an intervening God—a tautology based on faith, not science—he is simply wrong in arguing that without God there can be no scientific truth. There is scientific truth. Only time will tell whether Darwin's theory (or Einstein's or anyone else's) passes the demanding scientific tests of truth. But the existence or nonexistence of God is monumentally irrelevant to this issue of science.

Jefferson, too, was wrong in relying on "the Laws of Nature" for the moral basis of the rights asserted in the Declaration. He thought that he needed a source outside of the law as a trump, and at the time he was writing, natural law was that trump for people who rejected biblical law, as Jefferson did. Indeed, in those days, natural law was seen by more secular radicals, such as Rousseau, Spinoza, and Leibniz, as the progressive alternative to divinely revealed biblical law. Natural law was progressive in several senses: First, it was available to all who could observe nature and did not require Bibles, churches, prophets, priests, or government officials to translate or interpret the revealed word of God; second, its content was not fixed by the dead hand of the past, which all too often justified tyranny, authority, and repression; and third, these progressive proponents of natural law could infuse it with "better" natural rights, as Jefferson did with the right to secede and the rights of life, liberty, and the pursuit of happiness.

But today's more conservative proponents of natural law seek to infuse it with their own repressive values. Read how Alan Keyes uses the natural law of the Declaration of Independence to rail against homosexuality precisely because it may help gay men "pursue happiness":

And so once you have seen in the Declaration the logic that it defined, it is suddenly pretty clear that the first thing you have to remember is that freedom is not an unlimited license, it is not an unlimited choice, it is not even an unlimited opportunity. *Freedom* is, in fact, in the first instance, a responsibility. And it is in the first instance a *responsibility* before the God from whom we come. And now, see, I think that that has— once you start to think it through—tremendous consequences, because it also warns us against that understanding of rights which is based upon radical selfishness. You can't base rights on radical selfishness without asserting that *we are,* ourselves, *the source of those rights.* Once you have denied that, then radical selfishness becomes a contradiction of freedom. And those who then present to us the paradigm of family life, for instance—gay marriage and so forth. And people always say, "Well, what's wrong with that is that I disapprove of homosexuality." No. Let's leave that aside for the moment. I may disapprove of homosexuality. But from the point of view of public policy, what's wrong with it is that it is based upon an understanding of human sexuality that is radically selfish. By definition, I am in this relationship in order to gratify myself. Whereas, what? The foundation of the family is actually an understanding that in that relationship there is a necessary responsibility and obligation which transcends self-gratification in order to connect you with that which is your obligation to the child that may be born of it. You see? And so we can't accept it. Because if we go down that road we are rejecting the responsible understanding of freedom that is implied in the Declaration.

Keyes apparently confuses masturbation, which is self-gratification, with homosexuality, which, like heterosexuality, generally involves mutual gratification between partners, and often the responsibility of parenthood. He seems also to be unhappy about mutual gratification not designed for procreation, but even he cannot seriously argue that all harmless pleasures are inherently immoral—as distinguished from amoral—unless they affirmatively serve a noble purpose such as procreation.

To be sure, there are today also advocates of a variation on natural law who seek to infuse it with progressive values. Professor Ronald Dworkin, for example, eschews the phrase "natural law" as too metaphysical. Yet he argues that there are rights that transcend positive law and that can be "discovered" rather than invented. Primary among these rights is that governments must treat all citizens with equal concern and respect. Keyes would probably agree with that broad principle, but Dworkin and Keyes reach precisely the opposite conclusion as to how this equality principle applies to such issues as homosexuality, abortion, capital punishment, teaching evolution and mandating prayer in public schools, and most other agenda-driven disputes in the culture war that divides the Religious Right from the more secular left. In other words, we all agree that equality *should be* a governing consideration; advocates of natural law—from the right and the left alike—think it is a right that can be discovered; I think, however, that it is an important human invention based on our experiences with inequality and that it should be entrenched in the positive law. Yet, as I have shown, there is little agreement on what this "discovery" or "invention" mandates when it comes to some of the most divisive issues of the day, such as affirmative action or abortion rights. This is not to deny that a consensus regarding equality is important. It is. It marks an important signpost on the road of human development and experience. Based on this consensus, no one who subscribed to the principle of equality could today support slavery, a caste system, overt religious or gender discrimination, and other manifestations of blatant inequality. But that would be true today whether we believed equality came from God, Nature, or human experience. Indeed, those who believe it comes from God or Nature, rather than experience, have a burden to explain why the evils of inequality persisted for so long with the apparent blessing of God and Nature.

If equality—or any other right—came from God or Nature, it would be less subject to evolution than it quite obviously has been. "The laws of Nature and of Nature's God" are not supposed to change. They are supposed to be immutable. God the Creator does not bungle, and then have to correct his mistakes. But the only thing immutable about laws is that they are always changing, hopefully for the better. The farther away we have gotten from God's revealed law, the better the laws have gotten in regard to slavery, gender inequality, freedom, and justice. The more the laws try to control the evils in human nature (within limits, of course), the better these laws serve a higher morality.

The crowning irony is that some advocates of natural law now cite the Declaration of Independence as positive law, establishing natural law as part of our legal system. The problem, of course, is that even positive law cannot make something out of nothing—or bring into existence something that does not exist. Any attempt to establish natural law through positive law would be like enacting a statute seeking to amend Newton's law of gravity.

What, then, is the source of higher morality if it is not God's revealed word, or "the Laws of Nature and of Nature's God"? It is human experience! Trial and error! We are at our best when we recognize our past mistakes and try to build a better system of morality to avoid repetition of these mistakes! Rights come from wrongs! As Santayana observed, "Those who cannot remember the past are condemned to repeat it." A corollary to that astute observation is that understanding our past mistakes is a prerequisite to avoiding their repetition. Our present system of rights is not based on Nature or God, but rather on a recognition of our past wrongs and a desire not to repeat them—or do worse. We may attribute these ever-changing rights to God or Nature, but unless God changes His mind as often as people do, or unless He learns from His own mistakes, His name—and that of Nature—is being invoked in vain simply to add authority to changes based on human experience and reason.

Although the Declaration is remembered for its opening paragraphs filled with rhetorical flourishes about God-given unalienable *rights*, most of its words are about human *wrongs*. It was the wrongs committed against the colonists by the king, and those representing him, that were the stimuli to secession. It was the British wrongs that inspired the Americans to claim their own rights.

Rights Come from Wrongs

The Declaration's recitation of wrongs began with a general accusation: "The History of the present King of Great-Britain is a History of repeated Injuries and Usurpations, all having in direct Object the Establishment of an absolute Tyranny over these States." It then continues with a bill of particulars in the form of "Facts . . . submitted to a candid World." These facts—many of which were disputed by British lawyers and politicians as well as by some American Tories—were stated in tendentious and somewhat conclusory terms. Historians have disagreed about the validity of particular allegations, but there is widespread agreement that the essence of the complaint was valid: namely, that the colonists were being denied the right to self-determination and self-governance, and that the consequence was a despotism that was anything but benevolent.

What is noteworthy—and enduring—about the catalog of wrongs is how so many of them relate to the rights subsequently enshrined in the Constitution and its first ten amendments. Among the wrongs was denial of trial by jury, lack of an independent judiciary, transfer of defendants to distant places for trial, the quartering of troops during peacetime, and the superiority of military over civil power. All of these wrongs were remedied by constitutional rights—some structural, some particular. What is surprising is that other notorious wrongs that were also addressed in the Constitution—such as general searches and the punishment of dissent—were not included in the Declaration of Independence.

When I argue that rights come from wrongs, I do not mean to suggest that the wrongs themselves inevitably produce rights. If Nazi Germany had won World War II, it is uncertain whether Jews would have had any rights. But Germany lost, and many rights—beginning with the Nuremberg trials—were recognized in reaction to the Nazi wrongs. The relationship between wrongs and rights may perhaps be analogized to that between an infection and the production of antibodies. An infection, like a wrong, often stimulates the production of antibodies that then protect against recurrence. Positive rights are political antibodies to a recurrence of wrongs. Our experience with human wrongs often acts as a stimulus for the recognition and entrenchment of new rights. This process requires human intelligence and an ability to learn from our experiences. The wrongs serve as stimuli to human reason and action. This combination often results in the recognition of new rights or a renewed appreciation and enforcement of old ones.

How Can Conflicting Rights Be Resolved?

Natural law also poses a serious problem when one right comes into conflict with another. If rights come directly from Nature or Nature's God, as Jefferson believed, how are conflicting claims of rights supposed to be resolved? This was an especially difficult question for deists, who believed in a nonintervening God who reveals his rules through the silent workings of Nature. Even if Nature were to speak, it would speak with a forked tongue. It tells one group of people that it favors a woman's right to choose abortion, and another group of people that it opposes all abortion. It says to some that homosexuality, masturbation, premarital sex, and non-missionary-position intercourse are all unnatural, while to others that any legal restrictions on consensual adult sex are unnatural. It tells the members of the National Rifle Association that they have the right to bear arms, while it tells supporters of the Brady Bill that they have a right to control and regulate the possession of guns.

A nonintervening God and a silent Nature cannot be expected to answer questions about what they really think of these competing claims of right. Nor did Jefferson and his colleagues trust the words of priests, prophets, or oracles who claim to know God's answer. For Jefferson, the practical resolution of this problem lay in government based on the consent of the governed: "to secure these [unalienable and God-given] Rights, Governments are instituted among Men, deriving their just Powers from the Consent of the Governed." But what if a majority of the governed consent to an action that a minority believes is in violation of "the Laws of Nature and Nature's God"? What if the governmental institution selected to resolve certain conflicting claims of right—say, the U.S. Supreme Court—resolves it in a way that many believe violates "the Laws of Nature and of Nature's God"? Jefferson's only answer—short of one side persuading the other to change its mind—appears to be physical force, that is, revolution, though not "for light and transient causes." The Declaration states: "whenever any Form of Government becomes destructive of these Ends, it is the Right of the People to alter or to abolish it." If this is the case, then who decides whether a majority of the governed have "become destructive of these Ends"? Who decides whose claim of right prevails? If the answer is the stronger in battle, then might would indeed make right—or at least determine whose "right" prevailed. This is surely a less than satisfying resolution, especially for those who believe in an orderly world in which justice, rather than might, should prevail.

A perfect example of conflicting claims of right—at least to the signers of the Declaration of Independence—revolved around the issue of slavery. Many colonialists believed that the right to own property was natural and

God-given, and that African slaves were property. They pointed to the Bible in support of slave ownership and to the "natural" differences between whites and blacks and the "superiority" of the former over the latter. Others believed that all people, including black slaves, were created equal and that slavery was a violation of "the Laws of Nature and of Nature's God." Moreover, a majority of voters—a category that did not include blacks—in most states clearly favored slavery, while an evolving majority in others probably did not.

How then should these conflicts—between different conceptions of natural law and different majorities—be resolved? As we will see in chapter 3, they were prudentially resolved by postponement, indecision, compromise— and eventually by a U.S. Supreme Court decision (in the *Dred Scott* case) that many believe was in violation of "the Laws of Nature and Nature's God." This led to the use of force. Might and right turned out to be on the same side in the Civil War, but, sadly, it does not always turn out that way. Had force not been employed, or had the wrong side won, slavery probably would still have been abolished— but much later—as a result of a changing moral consensus based on a recognition of the wrongness of slavery. This recognition grew out of our collective experiences with the evils of that institution: the wrongs of slavery eventually would have led to the right to be free from it. But these wrongs were not "self-evident" to all the signers of the Declaration of Independence, and neither was the right to be free from slavery, as we will see from focusing on the most significant change made in Jefferson's draft by Congress—the striking of the following paragraph from the draft approved by the five-man drafting committee:

He [King George III of Great Britain] has waged cruel war against human nature itself, violating its most sacred right of life & liberty in the persons of a distant people, who never offended him, captivating and carrying them into slavery in another hemisphere, or to incur miserable death in their transportation thither. This piratical warfare, the opprobrium of *infidel* powers, is the warfare of the *Christian* king of Great Britain. Determined to keep open a market where MEN should be bought & sold, he has prostituted his negative for suppressing every legislative attempt to prohibit or to restrain this execrable commerce: and that this assemblage of horrors might want no fact of distinguished die, he is now exciting those very people to rise in arms among us, and to purchase that liberty of which *he* also obtruded them; by murdering the people upon whom *he* also obtruded them; thus paying off former crimes committed against the *liberties* of one people, with crimes which he urges them to commit against the *lives* of another.

The history and fate of these remarkable words speak volumes about whether rights come from "the Laws of Nature and Nature's God" or whether they are largely a product of the very human processes of evaluating differing experiences over time and place, and effectuating political compromises to achieve tolerable consensus.

3

How Can Jefferson's Views of Equality and Slavery Be Reconciled?

Against Slavery, against Immediate Abolition

Perhaps no image captures the contradictions of Jefferson and his Declaration better than Garry Wills's description of the arrival at Philadelphia of the man who would soon pen the immortal words that "all Men are created equal" and the stricken paragraph that characterized slavery as "cruel war against human nature itself":

> Mr. Jefferson attended the Revolution in his finest coach and pants. Riding postillion was his slave, Jesse, while Richard attended his person. A third may

have cared for his baggage and the other two horses in Jefferson's train.

At about the time he drafted the Declaration, Jefferson owned more than 180 slaves. By 1822 he owned 267 slaves. His first memory "was of being carried on a pillow by a slave." His beloved home in Monticello was constructed by slaves. His final resting place would be in a coffin made by a slave carpenter. Slavery was integral to every aspect of his life. Even putting aside the emotionally laden—and ultimately unanswerable—question of whether Jefferson actually fathered children with his slave Sally Hemming, Jefferson's personal views on slavery, abolition, segregation, and the intellectual and moral "equality" of blacks are as daunting in their complexity as the racism of some of his views is evident in its simplicity.

When I was in high school we were told that the longest word in the English language was "antidisestablishmentarianism." This was before anyone ever heard of "supercalifragilisticexpialidocious," but the former is a real word and represented an important movement in England during the nineteenth century. Antidisestablishmentarians were those people who might not have favored the establishment of the Church of England as an initial matter. But now that it had been established for so many years, they feared that the act of disestablishing a church might convey an antireligious message. Jefferson's views of slavery were analogous, at least in one respect. He despised slavery and would have opposed its adoption anywhere in the world. He also opposed its spread to any area where it was not then practiced. But he did not support its immediate abolition in places where slavery had become part of accepted folkways, fearing that freeing the slaves and allowing them to live side by side with whites would result in a race war, with better-armed and better-trained whites slaughtering the former slaves, but with many white deaths as well. He pointed to the "deep-rooted prejudices entertained by the whites" and the "ten thousand recollections, by the blacks of the injuries they have sustained," as well as "new provocations," and "the real distinctions which Nature has made." He feared "convulsions which will probably never end but in the extermination of one or the other race." Yet he worried that if "something is not done and soon done, we shall be the murderers of our own children." His tragic prediction came true during the Civil War, though the descendants of his contemporaries were killed not by black Southerners but by white Northerners. Beyond that, of course, there were several slave uprisings in which blacks and whites died before the Civil War, but in far fewer numbers than the enormous casualties sustained in the War between the States. In regard to slavery, therefore, Jefferson was an antidisestablishmentarianist, as contrasted with his firm prodisestablishmentarian position on the Church of England.

One of the keys to reconciling Jefferson's antislavery and antiabolition views lies in how he understood the phrase "all Men are created equal." For Lincoln, fourscore and seven years after the Declaration of Independence, these words could mean only one thing: the immediate and total abolition of slavery throughout the South. For Jefferson, these same words were consistent with the perpetuation of slavery—at least for a time—in places where it had long been practiced, especially considering what he predicted would be a catastrophic alternative. As he put it in 1820: "We have the wolf by the ears and we can neither hold him, nor safely let him go. Justice is in one scale, and self-preservation in the other." But it was human beings, not wolves, who were being enslaved by the chains of the law, and his "parchment protests" were not, as we shall see, matched by his deeds.

Were Blacks and Whites "Created Equal" in Jefferson's View?

For Jefferson, human beings were products of head and heart. The head was the repository of intelligence, while the heart was the focal point of morality. There can be no question that Jefferson did not believe that blacks and whites were created equal with regard to intelligence. He was what early twentieth-century academics would characterize as a "scientific racialist." Indeed, according to the historian Paul Finkelman, "Jefferson was the intellectual godfather of the racist pseudo-science of the American school of anthropology." He believed that scientific observation established two conclusions: (1) that blacks were not as intelligent as whites; and (2) that this racial hierarchy was a matter of nature, not nurture. Combining this set of beliefs with Jefferson's beliefs regarding God's role in creating the laws governing human nature, it would seem to follow that God deliberately created blacks intellectually inferior to whites. That was God's design—His perverse plan.

Jefferson's "scientific" evidence in support of this natural disparity was his own observations and the historical accounts of others. In Jefferson's only full-length book—*Notes on the State of Virginia*—he wrote the following about his observations of the physical characteristics of blacks:

> The first difference which strikes us is that of color. Whether the black of the Negro resides in the reticular membrane between the skin and scarf-skin, or in the scarf-skin itself; whether it proceeds from the color of the blood, the color of the bile, or from that of some other secretion, the difference is fixed in nature, and is as real as if its seat and cause were better known to us. And is this difference of no importance? Is it not the foundation of a greater or less share of beauty in the two races? Are not the fine mixtures of red and white, the expressions of every passion by greater or less suffusions of color in the one, preferable to that eternal monotony, which reigns in the countenances, that immovable veil of black which covers the emotions of the other race? Add to these, flowing hair, a more elegant symmetry of form, their own judgment in favor of the whites, declared by their preference of them, as uniformly as

is the preference of the Oran-utan for the black woman over those of his own species. The circumstance of superior beauty, is thought worthy attention in the propagation of our horses, dogs, and other domestic animals; why not in that of man? Besides those of color, figure, and hair, there are other physical distinctions proving a difference of race. They have less hair on the face and body. They secrete less by the kidneys, and more by the glands of the skin, which gives them a very strong and disagreeable odor. This greater degree of transpiration, renders them more tolerant of heat, and less so of cold than the whites. Perhaps, too, a difference of structure in the pulmonary apparatus, which a late ingenious experimentalist has discovered to be the principal regulator of animal heat, may have disabled them from extricating, in the act of inspiration, so much of that fluid from the outer air, or obliged them in expiration, to part with more of it.

He then proceeded to his observations of their activities:

They seem to require less sleep. A black after hard labor through the day, will be induced by the slightest amusements to sit up till midnight, or later, though knowing he must be out with first dawn of the morning. They are at least as brave, and more adventuresome. But this may perhaps proceed from a want of forethought, which prevents their seeing a danger till it be present. When present, they do not go through it with more coolness or steadiness than the whites. They are more ardent after their females, but love seems with them to be more an eager desire, than a tender delicate mixture of sentiment and sensation. Their griefs are transient.

He went on to discuss their mental capacity:

Comparing them by their faculties of memory, in reason, and imagination, it appears to me that in memory they are equal to the whites; in reason much inferior, as I think one could scarcely be found capable of tracing and comprehending the investigations of Euclid; and that in imagination they are dull, tasteless, and anomalous.

Jefferson then considered whether these differences were functions of nature or of nurture:

It will be right to make great allowances for the difference of condition, of education, of conversation, of the sphere in which they move. Many millions of them have been brought to, and born in America. Most of them, indeed, have been confined to tillage, to their own homes, and their own society; yet many have been so situated, that they might have availed themselves of the conversation of their masters; many have been brought up to the handicraft arts, and from that circumstance have always been associated with the whites. Some have been liberally educated, and all have lived in countries where the arts and sciences are cultivated to a considerable degree, and all have had before their eyes samples of the best works from abroad. The Indians, with no advantages of this kind, will often carve figures on their pages not destitute of design and merit. They will crayon out an animal, a plant, or a country, so as to prove the existence of a germ in their minds, which only wants cultivation. They astonish you with strokes of the most sublime oratory, such as prove their reason and sentiment strong, their imagination glowing and elevated. But never yet could I find that a black had uttered a thought above the level of plain narration; never saw even an elementary trait of painting or sculpture. In music they are more generally gifted than the whites with accurate ears for tune and time, and they have been found capable of imagining a small catch. Whether they will be equal to the composition of a more extensive run of melody, or of complicated harmony, is yet to be proved. Misery is often the parent of the most affecting touches in poetry. Among the blacks is misery enough, God knows, but no poetry.

Jefferson concluded, based on these observations as well as historical accounts of some white Roman slaves who had become poets and philosophers, that "it is not their condition then, but nature, which has produced the distinction." Jefferson was not alone among intellectuals in reaching this conclusion. Indeed, David Hume was "apt to suspect the Negroes to be naturally inferior to whites." Yet Jefferson, ever the empiricist and the scientist, offered the following caveat: "I advance it, therefore, as a suspicion only that the blacks, whether originally a distinct race, or made distinct by time and circumstances, are inferior to the whites in the endowments both of body and mind." Nor would he preclude the possibility that time would alter his views. "Whether further observation will or will not verify the conjecture, that nature has been less bountiful to them in the endowments of the head, I believe that in those of the heart she will be found to have done them justice."

There are three important points to be made about this conclusion. First is its tentative nature. He characterized his conclusion regarding black mental inferiority as "suspicion" and "conjecture" and left open the possibility that "further observation" may "not verify the conjecture." Yet it is significant that his "suspicion" pointed not in the direction of equality, or even inequality caused by condition, but instead in the direction of inherent intellectual inferiority. Second, he attributed the alleged disparity entirely to "nature" and never to "Nature's God," who created the laws of human nature. This is a common cop-out for many religious people—attributing the *positive* aspects of nature to God, but remaining silent about its *negative* consequences. What is significant about this pregnant omission is that it strongly suggests that Jefferson was unhappy about the conclusion to which his observations had driven him. He regarded the alleged mental inferiority of blacks as an unfortunate reality, and refused therefore explicitly to attribute it to the design of his perfect God of nature. As Wills puts it, it was a central tenet of deism that "God bungleth not." Because Jefferson, unlike some traditional Christians, could not attribute evil to "the devil," in whom he did not believe, he simply remained silent about God's responsibility for this unfortunate "natural" inequality. Finally, when it came to endowments "of the heart," which are less amenable to rigorous empirical comparisons, Jefferson believed that blacks and whites were equal—nature has "done them justice." Even when it came to morality, Jefferson purported to base his conclusion on empirical observations: "That disposition to theft with which they have been branded, must be ascribed to their situation, and not to any depravity of the moral sense. The man in whose favor no laws of property exist, probably feels himself less bound to respect those made in favor of others."

In light of Jefferson's observations with regard to blacks, and the mixed conclusions he drew from his observations, it would be interesting to speculate about Jefferson's feelings toward women (not to mention black women). The men of the Enlightenment were convinced that although women have many virtues, they were not the equal of men with regard to reasoning, literary output, artistic accomplishment, and the like. Few of them could be "found capable of tracing and comprehending the investigations of Euclid," according to the conventional male wisdom of Jefferson's time. In a letter to Albert Gallatan in 1807, Jefferson observed that "the appointment of a woman to office is an innovation for which the public is not prepared, nor am I." The status of white women, especially white married women, was in many ways akin to that of slaves, but in other ways it was very different. Among southern aristocrats she was placed on a pedestal. As recently as 1964, the Georgia Supreme Court could say the following about "their" women:

> We believe the history of no nation will show the high values of woman's virtue and purity that America has shown. We would regret to see the day when this freedom loving country would lower our respect for womanhood or lessen her legal protection for no better reason than that many or even all other countries have done so. She is entitled to every legal protection of her body, her decency, her purity and good name.

The men of the Court then characterized the sexual "purity" of women as "the most precious attribute of mankind." It did not follow from this "high value" placed on women's virtue that they were entitled to equal pay or equal opportunity in the workplace, but at least there was no threat of warfare and slaughter if women were emancipated.

"Nature's God" did, then, create all men equal in the most important aspect of their endowment: their moral capacity. Garry Wills has observed that although "our culture takes reason and intellect to be the highest of man's faculties," for Jefferson and those who influenced him, the heart was more important than the head:

> Thus when Jefferson says that blacks are equal to whites in "benevolence, gratitude and unshaken

fidelity," he is listing the cardinal virtues of moral-sense theory, the central manifestations of man's highest faculty.

In 1809 Jefferson wrote to his friend Henry Gregoire that "talent" is not a measure of a person's "rights," invoking Isaac Newton, who, although "superior to others in understanding, he was not therefore lord of the person or property of others."

From his pseudoscientific observations, Jefferson derived false empirical conclusions as well as erroneous policy judgments. As the historian William Cohen summarized Jefferson's views:

The entire body of Jefferson's writings shows that he never seriously considered the possibility of any form of racial coexistence on the basis of equality and that from at least 1778 until his death, he saw colonization as the only alternative to slavery.

Though his views may well have been internally consistent—as Wills has argued—they still have failed the test of experience over time because they rested on erroneous premises. The eminent historian John Hope Franklin believes that this was inevitable:

It would seem hardly likely that anyone with such pronounced views on the inferiority of blacks, who at the same time, believed blacks and whites could not live together as free persons could entertain a deeply serious belief that slaves should be emancipated.

Jefferson's view of blacks as morally equal but intellectually inferior to whites led him to the conclusion that blacks should be treated paternalistically by whites. On one occasion he even analogized the freeing of a slave to abandoning a child. He elaborated this patronizing view as follows:

> My opinion has ever been that, until more can be done for them, we should endeavor, with those whom fortune has thrown on our hands, to feed and clothe them well, protect them from ill usage, require such reasonable labors only as is performed voluntarily by freemen, and be led by no repugnance to abdicate them, and our duties to them. The laws do not permit us to turn them loose, if that were for their own good; and to commute them for other property is to commit them to those whose usage of them we cannot control.

What Jefferson meant by "until more can be done for them" has engendered much controversy over the years.

Did Jefferson Want to Stop the Slave Trade?

Though it seems clear to historians that Jefferson was opposed to the slave trade, what remains unclear are the real reasons underlying this opposition. It seems that his early opposition to the slave trade was at least in part based on his opposition to British rule of the colonies. The historian John C. Miller writes that as Jefferson saw it:

The eradication of slavery was to be the crowning achievement of the American Revolution; that revolution could not be considered complete, he insisted, until this ugly scar, a vestige of the colonial period, had been removed.

Jefferson had good reason to associate the slave trade with the Crown's despotic rule. Two years before the Declaration of Independence, he supported a Virginia law that would have stopped the importation of slaves into that colony, but the king vetoed it. Jefferson wrote critically of that veto—or "negative"—arguing that before the "slaves we have" can be enfranchised, "it is necessary to exclude all further importations from Africa." In his 1776 draft of the Virginia Constitution he wrote that "no person hereafter coming into [Virginia] shall be held in slavery under any pretext whatever." Then in his draft of the Declaration of Independence, he wrote the paragraph that was eventually stricken by Congress that blamed George III for keeping open "a market where MEN should be bought & sold." He believed that this "execrable commerce" violated the "most sacred right of life & liberty" of those "distant people" who had "never offended" the king, thus strongly implying that African blacks—along with whites— were endowed by their Creator with this "sacred right," despite their legal status in Virginia and other colonies as the property of other men. Miller even speculates that Jefferson left "property" off the list of inalienable rights to set the stage for placing the human rights of the slaves above the property rights of slaveowners. Yet Jefferson's opposition to the continuation of slavery itself was much more ambivalent than his opposition to the slave trade. What was unambivalent, however, was his opposition to the exacerbation of the slavery problem through the importation of additional slaves, and Jefferson used this opposition as an opportunity to impugn the moral standing of the "Christian king" whom the colonists already believed was a tyrant.

The reasons why this powerful condemnation of George III was stricken from the draft tell an interesting story about the interplay among politics, economics, and morality in revolutionary America.

Why the Declaration Did Not Condemn the Slave Trade

Jefferson was outraged by the decision of the Continental Congress to strike the climactic paragraph condemning King George for continuing the slave trade. He blamed the "mutilation" of his draft on northern slave traders who wanted to continue to profit by selling slaves, as well as on South Carolinians and Georgians who felt they needed more slaves. But there was more to the story. The issues surrounding the slave trade and abolition were a complex blend of economic self-interest, moral ambivalences, and political realities.

For example, Jefferson's draft paragraph condemns the king for "exciting those very people to rise in arms among us, and to purchase that liberty of which *he* also obtruded them." This condemnation apparently refers to an offer made by the royal governor of Virginia in November 1775 to free any slaves belonging to rebels, if these slaves would join "his Majesty's troops . . . for more speedily reducing the Colony to a proper sense of their duty to his Majesty's crown and dignity." About a thousand slaves took the governor up on his offer and joined the British troops. But the Virginia militia defeated them, and the governor and his fleet left Virginia waters with the "property" of the patriots.

Was the British offer morally justified, morally unjustified, or simply an amoral and cynical attempt to use freedom as an inducement for military service? Certainly the slaves cannot be faulted for being unpatriotic to their owners or to a system that would keep them in bondage. John Adams was probably correct when he later wrote that although he was in favor of keeping Jefferson's slavery paragraph, he "thought the expression (as it came from Jefferson's pen) too passionate and too much like scolding, for so grave and solemn a document." There are other reasons as well for questioning Jefferson's passions on this divisive issue.

Jefferson was not alone, of course, among the signers of the Declaration in owning slaves. Fully one-third of the signers were slaveowners, and all of the original colonies permitted slavery. In fact, New York did not abolish slavery until 1827; New Jersey in the 1840s; and "John Jay revealed that 'the great majority' of Northerners accepted slavery as a matter of course." Without being too cynical, it is fair to point out that the positions taken by most of the signers reflected their own personal, regional, and political benefits. Jefferson's strong opposition to the continuation of the African slave trade was ideologically consistent with his Enlightenment politics and philosophy, but it also was entirely consistent with his economic self-interest. As several historians have noted, he had more than enough slaves, and "the African trade undermined the value of his slaves," but "the restricted supply kept slave prices high," and Jefferson sold slaves throughout his life to pay off his debts. His colony, Virginia, also had a surfeit of slaves not enjoyed by colonies such as South Carolina and Georgia. As Joseph J. Ellis summarized the economic situation:

> Jefferson knew from his experience in the House of Burgesses that many established slaveowners in the Tidewater region favored an end of imports because their own plantations were already well stocked and new arrivals only reduced the value of their own slave population.

Jefferson's political ambitions in Virginia were thus served by his opposition to the slave trade. Had he lived in South Carolina, he could not expect to be elected to statewide office if he opposed the slave trade. It is impossible to know what he would have advocated—or even believed—had he lived in South Carolina. Living in Virginia made it easier for Jefferson to reconcile his political and economic self-interest with his ideology and morality. His strong opposition to the slave trade was not a profile in courage, as was the action of Colonel John Laurens, who "jeopardized his political career in South Carolina" by strenuously supporting a program for freeing slaves by having them enlist in the army. But politicians, especially those who are young and not yet established in politics, are rarely heard of by history if they are as courageous as was Colonel Laurens. (Colonel who?)

The best proof that Jefferson did not act courageously with reference to the slavery issue lies in his own hypocritical refusal to compromise his economic self-interest, even when it was strikingly inconsistent with his "parchment protests."

Jefferson's Actions toward His Own Slaves Who Tried to Exercise Their "Inalienable Right to Liberty"

Some of Jefferson's own slaves tried to secure liberty and pursue happiness by escaping. Jefferson's response seems closer to that of Simon Legree than to that of William Lloyd Garrison: the historian William Cohen reports that when Jame Hubbard, a slave who worked at his plantation's nail factory, ran away, Jefferson had him apprehended. When he ran away again, Jefferson hired someone to return him, offering a bonus. When he was brought back in irons, Jefferson reported: "I had him severely flogged in the presence of his old companions." He was then imprisoned. Jefferson was convinced that Hubbard "will never again serve any man as a slave." Anticipating that as soon as he was released from jail he would again try to escape, Jefferson tried to protect his investment by selling the determined black man before he could make his getaway. But Hubbard foiled his plan by escaping before he could be sold. Cohen writes, "Throughout his life Jefferson hired slave catchers and asked his friends to keep an eye peeled for his thralls when they struck out for freedom." Over the years when Jefferson was the master of Monticello, more than forty of his slaves tried to run away. As early as 1769, he advertised in the local newspaper seeking the return of a runaway slave. He apparently emancipated only two slaves, one of whom purchased his freedom, and failed to free his slaves upon his death, as George Washington, John Randolph, George Wythe, and others had done. His apparent excuse was that he was strapped for cash, but that was the result of his selfish choice to live a life of extravagant luxury at the expense of his slaves. Although he wrote that "nothing is more certainly written in the book of fate than that these people are to be free" and he believed that they had "a natural right" to seek their freedom, he was determined to thwart fate and defy nature when his own pocketbook was at stake. Here we do not see any clash of principles but simply a crass cost-benefit analysis entirely incompatible with Jefferson's announced principles. Even if Jefferson was convinced that blacks could not live as free and equal citizens among whites, that would not justify his repressive attempts to stop them from making their own decision to endure the risks of freedom.

Jefferson's Slave Code

Neither did Jefferson show a manifest interest in the well-being of the slaves when he worked to revise his state's slave code. Shortly after drafting the Declaration of Independence, Jefferson was selected to serve on a committee of Virginians to revise the statutes of that state—a task that took two years to complete. Although he claimed that the revised statutes constituted a "mere digest" of existing law, there were numerous changes and an opportunity to suggest others. Yet the provisions of the code dealing with slavery remained entirely consistent with Jefferson's property interest in slaves, and inconsistent with his expressed philosophy about their "natural right" to seek their freedom. While strengthening Virginia's prohibition against the continuing African slave trade, it maintained the slaveholder's total control over his property.

Under the revised code, a slave still could be whipped for running away—a provision Jefferson took full advantage of in dealing with his own runaways—or for making "seditious speeches," rioting, or other slave offenses. There were some changes, such as a prohibition against "free Negroes" entering or remaining in Virginia. The penalty for violating this prohibition was "outlawry"—being placed "out of the protection of the law," which meant that he or she could be killed or reenslaved.

So anxious were the Virginians about any increase in the number of blacks—slave or free—in their state, that their new code also provided that any white woman who gave birth to a black child must leave and take her baby with her or they would be outlaws. According to Cohen, Jefferson apparently "feared that a sizable population of free Negroes would be an incitement to unrest among the slaves." He pointed to the slave revolt in Santo Domingo and warned that "it is high time we should face the bloody scenes which our children certainly and possibly ourselves . . . [will] have to wade through, and try to avert them." Identifying with the former slaveowners who had been driven from Santo Domingo by their former slaves, Jefferson urged that they be welcomed into the United States and that the state of Virginia make a large donation to these refugees. He described the plight of the former slaveowners with the hyperbolic exclamation that there "never was so deep a tragedy presented to the feelings of men," suggesting that it was even greater than the tragedy of the slavery that led to the revolt itself.

Jefferson's Plan for Separate but Equal Freedom

While preserving the value of his own slaves and his ability to maintain control over them, Jefferson did try to remain consistent with his philosophy when it did not impinge on his own self-interest. In addition to opposing the continuation of the slave trade with Africa—which, pursuant to a constitutional compromise, was allowed to continue until 1808—Jefferson also generally opposed the expansion of slavery to new states and territories. He also formulated plans for the very gradual elimination of slavery in the slave states.

In his *Notes on the State of Virginia,* Jefferson described one of the plans:

> To emancipate all slaves born after the passing the act . . . and farther directing, that they should continue with their parents to a certain age, then to be brought up, at the public expense, to tillage, arts, or sciences, according to their geniuses, till the females should be 18, and the males 21 years of age, when they should be colonized to such place as the circumstances of the time should render most proper, sending them out with arms, implements of household and of the handicraft arts, seeds, pairs of the useful domestic animals, etc., to declare them a free and independent people, and extend to them our alliance and protection, till they have acquired strength; and to send vessels at the same time to other parts of the world for an equal number of white inhabitants; to induce them to migrate hither.

Jefferson understood how impractical this scheme would be to a financially strapped slave society. In 1824 he wrote that resettling a million and a half slaves in Africa would not be "practicable for us, or expedient for them":

> Their estimated value as property, in the first place, (for actual property has been lawfully vested in that form, and who can lawfully take it from the possessors?) at an average of two hundred dollars each . . . would amount to six hundred millions of dollars

which must be paid or lost by somebody. To this add
the cost of their transportation by land and sea to
Mesurado, a year's provision of food and clothes,
implements of husbandry and of their trades, which
will amount to three hundred millions more . . . and
it is impossible to look at the question a second time.

He proposed instead that newborn slaves be sent to Santo
Domingo, which had offered to accept them. But he
insisted that the federal government pay twelve dollars and
fifty cents to the slaveowners for each newborn, and that it
pay for their "nurture with the mother [for] a few years."
The young blacks would then have to work for their own
maintenance before being shipped off to Santo Domingo,
which would bear the cost of transportation.

These were but two of several plans Jefferson considered
throughout his lifetime, all of which had several factors in
common:

- Abolition would be gradual and would almost certainly not apply to his own slaves, though it would to
their children.

- The free slaves would not remain in Virginia, but
would be "colonized" elsewhere. "It is certain," he
wrote, "that these two races equally free cannot live
in the same government."

- The federal government would bear some financial
responsibility for the transition between slavery and
freedom. Former slaves would not simply be
deported with no resources.

Of course, none of these harebrained schemes worked, and there are those who suspect that Jefferson knew they were pie in the sky, and proposed them to show that deep down he was, at least in theory, an abolitionist, and to buy time for the perpetuation of slavery until political, economic, and social conditions doomed it as an immoral anachronism.

Though Jefferson's views on slavery sound bizarre to the contemporary ear, they did not depart unduly from the perspective shared by other "liberal" slaveowners, particularly in Virginia. (His inaction, however, in refusing to free his own slaves did differ markedly from at least some Virginians.) Over time, Jefferson's contradictory views on slavery would be condemned by slaveholders and abolitionists alike.

Conclusion

Professor Garrett Ward Sheldon has summarized Jefferson's inconsistencies with regard to slavery as follows:

> In the end, Jefferson's ideas and actions on slavery, within the context of his political philosophy, may tell us more about the human capacity for self-deception than anything else.

I believe it tells us something far more profound. It demonstrates the absurdity of any claim that rights (or law, or morality) come from "the Laws of Nature and of

Nature's God," that they are unalienable, or that they are self-evident. Rights come from fallible human beings struggling to prevent the recurrence of wrongs perpetrated by other human beings. Rights are human inventions, not supernatural or natural truths waiting out there—like a distant planet—to be discovered or revealed. They are certainly not absolute, immutable, or unalienable. Our long history demonstrates that they change with human experience and with the political, economic, cultural, and religious views of the age.

Slavery is the perfect example of this process in operation. God's revealed law authorizes slavery. Slaves are mentioned twice in the full version of the Ten Commandments, and the biblical rules regulating slavery are as detailed as Jefferson's slave code (though somewhat more benign). There is no way around the conclusion that the God of the Bible (or the men who wrote in His name) encouraged slavery. John Calhoun correctly cited the Bible in support of Patriarch Abraham's "extended household" filled with slaves "under the firm authority of its male" as the paradigm of biblical family organization. Some apologists for slavery even claimed that there was a Christian "right" to be a slave. Human nature, too, accepted slavery for more than 95 percent of recorded history. Accordingly, it was argued that slavery was "the natural and proper condition of all labor."

Yet slavery is wrong. God was wrong, the Bible is wrong, and human nature has been wrong for thousands of years about slavery.

Now, suddenly, all decent people recognize that this

enduring institution—blessed by God, popes, rabbis, ministers, and those who purported to know Nature's message—is deeply immoral and violates the most fundamental human rights. Why the sudden change? Has there been a new revelation? I guess I must have missed it. Has Nature changed? Not that I have noticed. Have we just gotten smarter and better able to understand the constant message of God and Nature? I doubt it. But something has indeed changed. We have learned from our terrible experiences with slavery that it is wrong. We have seen what it does to people, both slaves and slaveholders. Whites have gotten to know blacks on a more equal basis, and can see how wrong Jefferson was about their inherent abilities. The right not to be a slave would be a mere abstraction if we had not experienced the wrong of slavery. Rights come from wrongs, not from God or Nature, and they will continuously change and develop as long as human beings remain as ingenious as we have been in inventing new wrongs to inflict on our fellow human beings. Humanity will survive if our capacity to invent and enforce rights stays ahead of our capacity to invent and inflict wrongs. We will not endure if our capacity to invent and inflict wrongs destroys our capacity to respond with rights.

Jefferson's attempt to translate Nature directly into unalienable (and therefore unchangeable) rights, without the intermediation of changing human experience over time, demonstrates an inherent fallacy of natural law. Putting aside the reality that perceived truth changes with experience, even if it were true that blacks as a group (or women or Jews) were naturally "inferior" to others (which others?), it would still not follow that their rights should be inferior. It might even follow that they should have greater rights, to level the playing field. The contentious arguments regarding affirmative action combine empirical assertions—both short- and long-term—with normative moral claims. Translations from *is* to *ought* are always problematic, especially because such translations, were they to become the norm, would encourage special pleaders to reach distorted factual conclusions that support the moral judgments they seek to reach. Nazi racial "science" was a perfect example of this dangerous phenomenon at work. Jefferson's racial "science," though far more benign in its intentions, also produced malignant results.

The rhetoric of divine rights, natural rights, and unalienable rights is—and generally has been—a tactic employed to try to keep us ahead of wrongs, other than when it was used to justify monarchy and repression under the rubric of the divine or natural right of kings. But it is a tactic whose time has passed. I don't know whether Jefferson believed in this rhetoric when he wrote it into the Declaration of Independence. His actions with regard to slavery would suggest that he may not have, or that if he did, he did not act on his beliefs. But if he did believe it, he was wrong, and the fact that he put "the Laws of Nature and of Nature's God" into our Declaration of Independence does not make them real, any more than the fact of angels being in the Bible makes them real. Human beings such as Jefferson were responsible for perpetuating slavery, and human beings such as Jefferson were responsible for sowing the seeds that allowed other human beings, such as Lincoln, to end slavery. The Declaration of Independence was wrong in crediting "the Laws of Nature and of Nature's God" for our rights. The Declaration was correct in crediting our rights to "Governments . . . instituted among Men, deriving their just Powers from the Consent of the Governed." It's about time we acknowledged our own responsibility for both rights and wrongs.

Conclusion

What conclusions can the twenty-first-century world derive from the words of the Declaration of Independence written more than two and a quarter centuries ago by people who lived in a different world in which their words had different meanings? Very general and cautious ones only!

There are grave risks in drawing specific, agenda-driven conclusions about today's divisive issues from yesterday's differently understood words. Though the "skin" may look the same over the centuries, the "living thoughts" have changed with time and experience. What was "self-evident" to our forefathers may be subject to challenge today, and what appears self-evident to us may be challenged by our progeny. Yet we need an enduring structure of rules and rights for a government to survive as long, and as successfully, as ours has. Words are weak vessels indeed to convey the complexity of human experience and thought, but they are all we have. Locke reminded us that words are "the signs of our ideas only." And when we "clothe an idea in words," it may lose "its freedom of movement." I do not subscribe to the reductionist proclamation that Lewis Carroll placed in the mouth of Humpty Dumpty that "when I use a word, it means what I choose it to mean—neither more nor less." That would turn language into individualized ciphers incapable of general application. Words have accepted meanings—at any given point in time. Sometimes, if they are general or ambiguous, they are merely a cover for our inability to agree or decide. As Goethe quipped, "when an idea is wanting, a word can always be found to take its place."

The Declaration of Independence used ambiguous words such as "equal" and "rights" because a consensus regarding slavery was wanting. But these words have changed their color and texture over the centuries and have survived to inspire new generations of people who have experienced life differently from our forbearers.

Justice Antonin Scalia recently characterized the U.S. Constitution as a "dead" document. He rejects, as "the conventional fallacy," the idea that "the Constitution is a 'living document'"—that is, a text whose meaning may differ from generation to generation with changing experiences. Instead he believes the Constitution is "dead," in that it means precisely "what it meant when it was adopted." Scalia argues that such a mode of interpretation makes the Constitution more "enduring."

In reality, this viewpoint simply permits Scalia to impose an eighteenth-century view of law and life—a view that just happens to coincide with his personal, political, and religious philosophy—on the very different twenty-first-century world. In his world, a state could punish adultery by branding, horse stealing by hanging, and blasphemy by whipping. The states (but not the federal government) also could prohibit Catholics, like him, from serving as a judge or running for office, and could compel them to support the established Protestant church. The states probably could even censor some of the provocative and disturbing speeches Scalia has given. All this would be possible because the framers of the Constitution did not intend the Bill of Rights to impose limits on the states, and at the time the Constitution was written, several states did just those abominable things. Of course, no state today would enact such laws (well, maybe Texas would, if it could, still hang horse thieves!), but according to Scalia, if one did, it would be perfectly constitutional, since the meaning of the words of the Constitution—even the most general ones such as "due process," "cruel and unusual punishment," and "equal protection"—never change with our changing experiences.

The Scalia approach to textual interpretation, in addition to simply masking his personal preferences for an eighteenth-century world, reflects a basic misunderstanding of the function of language. Words cannot be meaningfully understood outside of the context and time frame in which they were written. If they are indeed "the signs of our ideas only," as Locke correctly said they were, then they cannot be understood without a full comprehension of the ideas of the time during which they were written. Scalia does not dispute this truism. His essential fallacy, however, is that he ignores the likelihood that those who drafted the Constitution understood better than he does that the meaning of words—especially some of the open-ended and general ones deliberately selected—inevitably change with time and experience. The framers may well have anticipated and intended that their words would be interpreted by future generations differently than they themselves may have understood them. That is why they wrote some provisions in rather open-ended and broad terms while employing narrow, more specific language for other provisions. It may well have been their *general intent* that their *specific intent* not place a dead hand on future generations. This certainly seems to have been the case with regard to whether blacks were persons who were entitled to the equal protection of the law, as distinguished from property that could only be taken from its owner for just compensation. There could be no agreement about that divisive issue, or about others surrounding the institution of slavery. Accordingly, compromises were reached. Some were specific—such as the precise date on which the African slave trade would be ended (twenty years after the ratification of the Constitution). Others were more general, such as the inclusion of equality language as a limitation on the federal government but not on the states. It is certainly possible—indeed, likely—that the words "due process" and "cruel and unusual punishment" were intended by their drafters to invite a change in content over time and with changing experiences. Yet Scalia ignores this likely scenario, and insists, with Humpty Dumpty, that when Madison and presumably Jefferson used a word it must be understood today to mean exactly what they "chose it to mean"—more than two centuries ago—"nothing more, nothing less."

To demonstrate the absurdity of the Scalia approach to the interpretation of words, let us consider what it would mean for the Declaration of Independence. I recognize, of course, that there are differences in the manner by which constitutions and declarations are interpreted. Scalia, however, seems to interpret all text—including biblical text—in a similarly "dead" manner.

The most memorable and oft-quoted words, phrases, and concepts of the Declaration of Independence have dramatically different meanings today than they did to those who wrote them in 1776.

Consider the following six phrases:

1. "The Laws of Nature and of Nature's God."
2. "We hold these Truths to be self-evident."
3. "All Men are created equal."
4. "Endowed by their Creator with certain unalienable Rights."
5. "Life, Liberty, and the Pursuit of Happiness."
6. "The Right of the People to alter or to abolish it . . . to throw off such Government."

"The Laws of Nature and of Nature's God"

In 1776 "the Laws of Nature and of Nature's God" had a precise, rather technical, meaning as well as a broader, more general understanding. As I have shown, to deists such as Jefferson it meant the nonintervening watchmaker who was the first cause, setting in motion the universe and establishing the rules of both physical and human nature. Does this mean that to be a patriotic American and believe in the "God of the Declaration"—paraphrasing Alan Keyes and George Bush—one would have to reject the God of the Bible, as Jefferson did? Or accept a watchmaker God who created some races with more inherent intelligence than others? Of course not. To the diverse array of Protestants who constituted the vast majority of colonial Americans, "Nature's God" probably meant a generic deity who transcended particular sects. To some it may have represented the Calvinist God of predestination, to others the very different Quaker or Unitarian divinity. Since there were few (or no) atheists, Catholics, Jews, Muslims, Buddhists, or members of other faiths in colonial America, there was no occasion to consider or resolve some of the most contentious issues that divide our far more heterogeneous population today. Just as our godless Constitution cannot be cited as proof that we are a godless people—as distinguished from a godless polity that separates church and state—so, too, our God-filled Declaration cannot properly be cited as proof that belief in God, or Christianity, is essential to good citizenship. Issues not confronted by our founding fathers cannot be deemed to have been resolved by their words. If words are the skins of living thoughts, then we must look beneath the surface of these skins to discern the changing meanings of common words.

The very concept of "the Laws of Nature and of Nature's God" has little meaning in today's world, where deism is dead, and the conflicts tend to be between those who believe in the revealed word of the Bible's God and those who believe in no God at all. Jefferson and many of his contemporaries rejected both of these views. More particularly, they rejected the former, because it had been the cause of so many wrongs, and they ignored the latter because, as Paine observed, there were no people who did not believe in some God. The debates of 1776 contribute little to resolving today's very different disputes except to suggest that the founding fathers—based on their experience—wanted to keep churches, clerics, and biblical revelations separate from the secular business of governance. To read much more into the reference to "the Laws of Nature and of Nature's God" is to read one's own contemporary preferences into words that cannot sustain these agendas.

"We Hold These Truths to Be Self-Evident"

In 1776 many scientists believed that bodies of "truth" were out there waiting to be discovered—and that once discovered, these truths were as "self-evident" as Newton's law of gravity. These transcendent and static bodies included not only physical truths but also moral truths, perhaps even legal truths. There was little dispute between science and morality (whether religiously based or not) about this conception. Today there are few reputable scientists who believe that moral or legal truths are comparable to physical or scientific truths. The entire vocabulary has changed, as we recognize that the "laws" of physics bear no relation—other than sharing a common word in *some* languages—to the "laws" of morality or the "laws" that are enacted by legislatures to govern our conduct. A poem written by Alexander Pope exemplifies this confusion:

> All are but parts of one stupendous whole,
> Whose body Nature is, and God the soul; . . .
> All Nature is but art, unknown to thee;
> All chance, direction, which thou canst not see;
> All discord, harmony not understood;
> All partial evil, universal good:
> And, spite of pride, in erring reason's spite,
> One truth is clear, whatever is, is right.

To the extent that Pope is referring to the "is" of physics or paleontology, he is tautologically correct, but no one other than an extreme defender of the status quo would agree that "whatever is" in politics, law, or morality is necessarily "right."

Many prominent legal scholars of the age—Blackstone was the most influential both in England and in the colonies—believed that the law was a truth to be discovered. Blackstone maintained that there are "eternal, immutable laws of good and evil, to which the creator himself in all his dispensations conforms; and which he has enabled human reason to discover, so far as they are necessary for the conduct of human actions." The American school of legal realism—beginning with Holmes and reaching its zenith in the mid-twentieth century—changed all of that. With few exceptions, no one today believes that the law is an abstraction in the sky rather than a human invention. "The life of the law," Holmes correctly observed, "has not been logic; it has been experience." And the implications of experience for "truth" are neither static nor self-evident. Experience, morality, legality, even truth are ever-changing, always adapting, constantly evolving reactions to nature and nurture. Experience, in my opinion, has made *evident* the need for the Declaration's rights, but when we now say they are *self-evident*, we most certainly do not mean it as Jefferson did.

"All Men Are Created Equal"

If the equality of "all Men" had any relevance to their rights, as Jefferson suggested they did, then these words could only have included white, Protestant, landowning males—since blacks, non-Protestants, nonlandowners, and women were denied some of the most basic rights we take for granted today. Some or all could not vote, serve on juries, hold public office, appear as witnesses, make contracts, or live freely. Either the word "equal" must have had a very different meaning then than it does today, or the words "all" and "Men" could not have meant what they now mean. Even the word "created" carries a different connotation in today's public discourse than it did in 1776. As evidenced by the words of Keyes and Falwell, to today's Religious Right it means acceptance of the biblical story of creation. To Jefferson's contemporaries it meant a deist God who set in motion the laws of biology that led to the development—"evolution" was not yet discovered—of human beings. Yet what is clear is that we should not consider the Declaration a useless weapon in the fight for civil rights and equality, especially for women and blacks, simply because its theory of equal creation means something different to us than it did to its authors.

"Endowed by Their Creator with Certain Unalienable Rights"

One rarely hears the word "unalienable"—or even Jefferson's original "inalienable"—spoken today. Experience has taught us that all rights are alienable. There is no right so basic that, under extraordinary circumstances, it will not—and should not—be alienated.

The law recognizes this reality in the law of "necessity"—a law twice cited in the Declaration itself: "When in the Course of human Events, it becomes necessary"; "We must, therefore, acquiesce in the Necessity . . ."

Scholars have long debated the legal and moral parameters of the necessity defense: Does it permit three starving sailors on a raft to hasten the inevitable death of a fourth so that they may survive? Would it justify the decision of fifty Jews hiding from Nazi pursuers in an attic to suffocate a crying baby to avoid being sent to Auschwitz? May a moral army bomb a terrorist hideout if it knows that along with killing the terrorist, they are likely to kill a small number of innocent civilians? May an orthodox Catholic doctor perform an abortion—and thus, in his view, end a life—to save the life of the mother? Is it ever permissible to torture someone—say, an admitted terrorist who knows where a ticking bomb is hidden, or a kidnapper who knows where your child is buried with only enough air to live for several hours?

In whatever way these and a myriad of other comparable choice-of-evil cases are resolved, there can be no doubt that no system of law or morality has ever, or will ever, succeed in defining rights that are "unalienable." The only question is whether to *say* they are unalienable, and then simply alienate them when necessary—or to acknowledge up front that they are alienable, and to define, with specificity, the conditions under which they may properly be alienated. As realistic jurisprudence has replaced the "law is there to be discovered" school of the eighteenth century, the trend—even in written constitutional documents such as the Canadian Charter of Rights and Freedoms—has been toward recognizing the alienability of rights, and the language of "unalienability" has become something of an anachronism. At the very least, it is clear that our experience with the alienability of certain rights during times of crisis requires us to alter our conception of the word "unalienable."

"Life, Liberty, and the Pursuit of Happiness"

In 1776 most of today's issues involving the "right to life"—such as capital punishment, abortion, and assisted suicide—were not on the political agenda. The death penalty was taken for granted by everyone except Quakers, and even they were satisfied to try to narrow the range of offenses to which it was applicable. This was a daunting task, especially since prisons—as we know them—had not yet been invented. There were jails and holding cells, but the large prisons designed for long confinement would have to await the Jacksonian era. Life imprisonment was not a realistic alternative to the death penalty, and dangerous criminals would either be executed or exiled (to become the problems of another society). The case for considering the death penalty as "cruel and unusual punishment" was much weaker than it is today, when mandatory life imprisonment is a realistic option and when execution has become far more "unusual," though perhaps less "cruel" in its implementation.

Abortion was not a "right to life" issue in 1776. Under English common law, which was controlling before the Declaration of Independence and remained influential even thereafter, abortion before "quickening" was not a crime. Most of the states did not pass laws banning abortions until the 1830s, despite the fact that "elective abortions were not unknown" even to colonial women. This suggests that abortion was not considered a pressing issue. In revolutionary America there was little debate about a fetus's right to life, and we can be relatively certain that the "right to life" was not interpreted to mean the right of a fetus not to be aborted, as it sometimes is today.

Suicide was a crime and a sin in 1776, though Jefferson was somewhat critical of treating it as such. Judge Robert R. Beezer of the Ninth Circuit, dissenting in a 1996 appellate case declaring a right to die, cited Jefferson's opposition to criminal sanctions on suicide as "presaging the sentiments of the drafters of the Model Penal Code." This is what Jefferson said:

> Men are too much attached to this life to exhibit frequent instances of depriving themselves of it. At any rate, the quasi-punishment of confiscation will not prevent it. For if one can be found who can calmly determine to renounce life, who is so weary of his existence here as rather to make experiment of what is beyond the grave, can we suppose him, in such a state of mind, susceptible to influence from the losses to his family by confiscation?"

The Jefferson who penned these words certainly cannot be cited by the Religious Right as supporting their view that the "unalienable" right to life meant that one could not take his or her own life because that right belonged to God. He somewhat mockingly stated that "if this is a 'Christian Nation,' then only God theoretically has the right to take a life. It's a touchy issue. I personally believe you have every right to suicide, but only if you succeed. Failures should be punished." If anything, Jefferson seemed to think that the right to one's life included the option to take it under dire circumstances, while he certainly did not believe it was trumped by any obligation to leave it to his nonintervening God.

The pursuit of happiness, too, had a rather technical meaning to Jefferson and those who influenced his thinking. Both Jefferson and Locke believed that "the pursuit of happiness" meant pursuit of long-term happiness through focus on "remote goods" such as "good conscience, good health, occupation, and freedom in all just pursuits." Not only does this contradict the often shortsightedly hedonistic practices that left Jefferson nearly bankrupt, but it also seems inapplicable to today's agenda issues such as smoking, drugs, and sexual freedom. Indeed, Jefferson's puritanical, even draconian views regarding homosexuality would undercut any claims that he supported an unrestricted right to seek happiness when that quest contradicted deeply held views about morality.

Putting aside the technical meaning of "pursuit of happiness," it is difficult to imagine a more open-ended word than "happiness." To limit it to its time-bound, late-eighteenth-century meaning for Jefferson and his fellow colonial Americans would be to rob it of all relevant meaning. What provides happiness for some people in our age may have been a source of misery for others in a different age. Being served by his slaves may have made Jefferson happy, but it would have made Lincoln—who famously said, "as I would not be a slave, so I would not be a master"—miserable. Killing animals for sport has made decent people happy for centuries. Yet I predict that before long, such killing will be deemed immoral by the consensus of decent opinion, and it will stop being enjoyable as we better understand the unnecessary pain we are inflicting on living beings. Happiness is a function of time, place, and experience. Pursuing it can never be permitted without limits. Your right to swing your fist ends at the tip of my nose, just as your right to pursue happiness by smoking ends at the entrance of my nostrils (or my home).

"The Right of the People to Alter or to Abolish It . . . to Throw Off Such Government"

In addition to endowing people—male people, white people?—with unalienable rights, some of which are enumerated, others not (*"among these* are Life, Liberty, and the Pursuit of Happiness" [emphasis mine]), the Declaration provides that if government were to become "destructive" of these rights, the people have an additional right: "to alter or to abolish it," "to throw off" the government, presumably by some armed violence, though they should not do so "for light and transient Causes."

These are, of course, some zealots who do read the revolutionary words of the Declaration literally. They form "militias" and "posies comitatus" and stand ready to overthrow the government if Congress enacts gun control laws that deprive them of their God-given, natural right to "bear arms." Timothy McVeigh cited Jefferson in justification for the necessity to murder children because he believed that our government had become destructive of his unalienable rights. Every revolutionary, anarchist, and terrorist believes he or she is obeying some higher natural law that takes precedence over positive law. To the extent that Jefferson intended his words to acknowledge an unalienable right to revolution, any such right would seem unsuited to a nation governed by democracy and the rule of law.

Most rational people do not read the words of the Declaration as Scripture. (Most rational people don't even read Scripture as Scripture; they understand that the meanings of even biblical words change with time and experience. For example, "adultery" in the Ten Commandments was limited to sexual intercourse involving a married woman— Clinton was right about that! Now everyone reads it as applying to married men as well.) The words of the Declaration were intended as a general "signal" rather than as fine print in a technical legal document. Its primary author intended these words as a "signal of arousing men to burst their chains under which monkish ignorance and superstition" had bound them. Signals are not meant to be read like contracts. Jefferson's "signal" explicitly contemplates the future. It would burst the chains in some parts of the world "sooner" and in "others later." Inevitably, its specific meaning would vary over time and place, with changing experiences and differing histories of wrongs.

Some Concluding Thoughts

If "hypocrisy is the homage that vice pays to virtue," as La Rochefoucauld quipped, then open-minded language, written deliberately to encourage broader future interpretation, is the homage that compromise pays to principle. The pragmatic drafters of our original documents of liberty understood the constraints under which they were writing. But they also understood that their resounding words could help break down these constraints when changing experiences freed their successors to do the right thing. Only by writing words that had one (hypocritical) meaning when written but that were capable of a different (more principled) meaning in the future could the framers accomplish their dual goals: achieving consensus for independence then, while signaling the hope to arouse men and women to a better world "sooner" or "later," when changing experiences warranted.

Justice Scalia is wrong to believe that a dead document is an enduring one. All that endures are empty words, shorn of context and contemporary relevance. Justice Arthur Goldberg was far wiser when he said that a living constitution must not be read "as if it were a last will and testament—lest it become one." The same can be said about the Declaration of Independence. Its ringing words should be read as its primary author intended—as a signal welcoming "the unbound exercise of reason and freedom of opinion" as well as the "light of science." Our Declaration should not be treated as a fragile parchment to be preserved under glass for fear that it might be damaged by contact with the light of today's and tomorrow's world. It should be handled with the care its age demands, but to assure that it remains a living and breathing document rather than a dead testament to the past, the Declaration of Independence must remain in constant use to inspire future generations to exercise their "reason and freedom," as it has inspired previous generations. If the historian Ralph Barton Perry is correct that "the history of American Democracy is the gradual realization, too slow for some and too rapid for others, of the implications of the Declaration of Independence," then as our history continues to unfold, in often unpredictable ways, we will continue to find new implications in this complex, yet enduring, document of freedom.

Appendix
The Declaration of Independence

IN CONGRESS, JULY 4, 1776.

A DECLARATION BY THE REPRESENTATIVES OF
THE UNITED STATES OF AMERICA, IN GENERAL
CONGRESS ASSEMBLED

When in the Course of human Events, it becomes necessary for one People to dissolve the Political Bands which
have connected them with another, and to assume among
the Powers of the Earth, the separate and equal Station to
which the Laws of Nature and of Nature's God entitle
them, a decent Respect to the Opinions of Mankind
requires that they should declare the causes which impel
them to the Separation.

We hold these truths to be self-evident, that all Men are
created equal, that they are endowed by their Creator with
certain unalienable Rights, that among these are Life, Liberty and the Pursuit of Happiness—That to secure these
Rights, Governments are instituted among Men, deriving
their just Powers from the Consent of the Governed, that

169

whenever any Form of Government becomes destructive of these Ends, it is the Right of the People to alter or to abolish it, and to institute new Government, laying its Foundation on such Principles, and organizing its Powers in such Form, as to them shall seem most likely to effect their Safety and Happiness. Prudence, indeed, will dictate that Governments long established should not be changed for light and transient Causes; and accordingly all Experience hath shewn, that Mankind are more disposed to suffer, while Evils are sufferable, than to right themselves by abolishing the Forms to which they are accustomed. But when a long Train of Abuses and Usurpations, pursuing invariably the same Object, evinces a Design to reduce them under absolute Despotism, it is their Right, it is their Duty, to throw off such Government, and to provide new Guards for their future Security. Such has been the patient Sufferance of these Colonies, and such is now the Necessity which constrains them to alter their former Systems of Government. The History of the present King of Great-Britain is a History of repeated Injuries and Usurpations, all having in direct Object the Establishment of an absolute Tyranny over these States. To prove this, let Facts be submitted to a candid World.

He has refused his Assent to Laws, the most wholesome and necessary for the public Good.

He has forbidden his Governors to pass Laws of immediate and pressing Importance, unless suspended in their Operation till his Assent should be obtained; and when so suspended, he has utterly neglected to attend to them.

He has refused to pass other Laws for the Accommodation of large Districts of people, unless those People would relinquish the Right of Representation in the Legislature, a Right inestimable to them, and formidable to Tyrants only.

He has called together Legislative Bodies at Places unusual, uncomfortable, and distant from the Depository of their Public Records, for the sole Purpose of fatiguing them into Compliance with his Measures.

He has dissolved Representative Houses repeatedly, for opposing with manly Firmness his Invasions on the Rights of the People.

He has refused for a long Time, after such Dissolutions, to cause others to be elected; whereby the Legislative Powers, incapable of Annihilation, have returned to the People at large for their exercise; the State remaining in the mean time exposed to all the Dangers of Invasion from without, and Convulsions within.

He has endeavoured to prevent the Population of these States; for that Purpose obstructing the Laws for Naturalization of Foreigners; refusing to pass others to encourage their Migrations hither, and raising the Conditions of new Appropriations of Lands.

He has obstructed the Administration of Justice, by refusing his Assent to Laws for establishing Judiciary Powers.

He has made Judges dependent on his Will alone, for the Tenure of their Offices, and the Amount and payment of their Salaries.

He has erected a Multitude of new Offices, and sent hither Swarms of Officers to harrass our People, and eat out their Substance.

He has kept among us, in Times of Peace, Standing Armies, without the consent of our Legislatures.

He has affected to render the Military independent of, and superior to the Civil Power.

He has combined with others to subject us to a Jurisdiction foreign to our Constitution, and unacknowledged by our Laws; giving his Assent to their Acts of pretended Legislation:

For quartering large Bodies of Armed Troops among us:

For protecting them, by a mock Trial, from Punishment for any Murders which they should commit on the Inhabitants of these States:

For cutting off our Trade with all Parts of the World:

For imposing Taxes on us without our Consent:

For depriving us, in many Cases, of the Benefits of Trial by Jury:

For transporting us beyond Seas to be tried for pretended Offences:

For abolishing the free System of English Laws in a neighbouring Province, establishing therein an arbitrary Government, and enlarging its Boundaries, so as to render it at once an Example and fit Instrument for introducing the same absolute Rule into these Colonies:

For taking away our Charters, abolishing our most valuable Laws, and altering fundamentally the Forms of our Governments:

For suspending our own Legislatures, and declaring themselves invested with Power to legislate for us in all Cases whatsoever.

He has abdicated Government here, by declaring us out of his Protection and waging War against us.

He has plundered our Seas, ravaged our Coasts, burnt our towns, and destroyed the Lives of our People.

He is, at this Time, transporting large Armies of foreign Mercenaries to complete the works of Death, Desolation, and Tyranny already begun with circumstances of Cruelty and Perfidy, scarcely paralleled in the most barbarous Ages, and totally unworthy the Head of a civilized Nation.

He has constrained our fellow Citizens taken Captive on the high Seas to bear Arms against their Country, to become the Executioners of their friends and Brethren, or to fall themselves by their Hands.

He has excited domestic Insurrections amongst us, and has endeavoured to bring on the Inhabitants of our Frontiers, the merciless Indian Savages, whose known Rule of Warfare, is an undistinguished Destruction, of all Ages, Sexes and Conditions.

In every stage of these Oppressions we have Petitioned for Redress in the most humble Terms: Our repeated Petitions have been answered only by repeated Injury. A Prince, whose Character is thus marked by every act which may define a Tyrant, is unfit to be the Ruler of a free People.

Nor have we been wanting in Attentions to our British Brethren. We have warned them from Time to Time of Attempts by their Legislature to extend an unwarrantable Jurisdiction over us. We have reminded them of the Circumstances of our Emigration and Settlement here. We have appealed to their native Justice and Magnanimity, and we have conjured them by the Ties of our common Kindred to disavow these Usurpations, which, would inevitably interrupt our Connections and Correspondence. They too have been deaf to the Voice of Justice and of Consanguinity. We must, therefore, acquiesce in the Necessity, which denounces our Separation, and hold them, as we hold the rest of Mankind, Enemies in War, in Peace, Friends.

We, therefore, the Representatives of the UNITED STATES OF AMERICA, in General Congress, Assembled, appealing to the Supreme Judge of the World for the Rectitude of our Intentions, do, in the Name, and by Authority of the good People of these Colonies, solemnly Publish and Declare, That these United Colonies are, and of Right ought to be, Free and Independent States; that they are absolved from all Allegiance to the British Crown, and that all political Connection between them and the State of Great-Britain, is and ought to be totally dissolved; and that as Free and Independent States, they have full Power to levy War, conclude peace, contract Alliances, establish Commerce, and to do all other Acts and Things which Independent States may of right do. And for the support of this declaration, with a firm Reliance on the Protection of Divine Providence, we mutually pledge to each other our lives, our Fortunes, and our sacred Honor.

Notes

INTRODUCTION

1 *[T]he independence* Pauline Maier, *American Scripture: Making the Declaration of Independence* (New York: Alfred A. Knopf, 1997), p. 95.

4 *a word is not* *Towne v. Eisner*, 245 U.S. 418, 425 (1918) (Holmes, J.).

5 *these United Colonies* David McCullough, *John Adams*, (New York: Simon & Schuster, 2001), p. 118.

6 *you can write* Ibid., p. 119.
obnoxious, suspected Ibid.
I consented Ibid.
Alone in his Ibid., pp. 120–121.

7 *originality of principle* Thomas Jefferson, *Letter to Henry Lee*, May 8, 1825, in *The Life and Selected Writings of Thomas Jefferson* (New York: Franklin Library ed., 1982), p. 577.
preoccupied with more Joseph J. Ellis, "The Enduring Influence of the Declaration," in Joseph J. Ellis, *What Did the Declaration Declare* (Boston: Bedford/St. Martin's, 1999), p. 18.

8 *to the world* Thomas Jefferson, *Letter to Roger C. Weightman*, June 24, 1826 (New York: Franklin Library ed.), p. 585.

1. WHO IS THE GOD OF THE DECLARATION?

9 *I would see no*   Edwards v. *Aguillard,* 482 U.S. 578, 606–607 (1987) (Powell, J., concurring).

10 *The ideal of the*   Anson Phelps Stokes, *Church and the State in the United States* (New York: Harper & Brothers, 1950), p. 462.

any diligent student   Jerry Falwell, *Listen, America!* (Garden City, N.Y.: Doubleday, 1980), p. 25.

The Founders actually   Jerry Falwell, "Founding Fathers— Liberty Alliance Article," August 10, 2000, www.mcbible. com.

11 *self-government by*   Anti-Defamation League, *The Religious Right: The Assault on Tolerance and Pluralism in America* (1994), pp. 4–6.

is Lord of the government   Ibid.

12 *Given this vast volume*   James Dobson, "Was America a Christian Nation?," 1996, www.cs.umanitoba.ca/jacobn/ jacobs/articles/dobson.html.

protecting America's Christian heritage and other quoted excerpts in this paragraph   *The Declaration of Independence and the Constitution of the United States of America* (Coral Ridge Ministries ed.), p. 63, www.coralridge.com.

Our rights   Senator Joseph Lieberman, *Meet the Press,* October 21, 2001.   The transcript is available at www. washingtonpost.com.

a bridge between   Alan Keyes, address to the Declaration Foundation, "*Declaration Principles Reborn,*" August 11, 1996. All his speeches are available in his archives at www.renewamerica.tv.

13 *some mechanistic deity* through *very personal God*   Alan Keyes, speech at the Calvary Church in Southern California, October 28, 2000.

He has started   Keyes, address to the Declaration Foundation, 1996.

is not, and cannot be Michael Novak, *God's Country: Taking the Declaration Seriously* (Washington, D.C.: AEI Press, 2000), pp. 16–17.

14 *the font and spring* Ibid., p. 7.

Jefferson twice referred Ibid., p. 15.

republic and *liberty* Ibid., p. 21.

ignorant, unlettered F. Forrester Church, "Foreword," in Thomas Jefferson, *The Jefferson Bible* (Boston: Beacon Press, 1989), p. 15.

so much absurdity Ibid., p. 28.

dung Jaroslav Pelikan, "Afterword," in Jefferson, *The Jefferson Bible*, p. 157.

15 *awkward monkish fabrication* Thomas Jefferson, "Appendix," in *Reports of Cases Determined in the General Court of Virginia from 1730 to 1740 and from 1768 to 1772* (Charlottesville, Va.: F. Carr and Co., 1829), p. 141.

laws made for the Jews Ibid., p. 142.

the one that trusteth Allen Jayne, *Jefferson's Declaration of Independence: Origins, Philosophy, and Theology* (Lexington: University of Kentucky Press, 1998), p. 16.

watchmaker God Ibid., p. 24.

16 *the government of the United States* Leo Pfeffer, *Church, State, and Freedom* (Boston: Beacon Press, 1967), p. 211.

As the heirs Maier, *American Scripture,* p. xix.

17 *The Judeo-Christian God* Peter M. Rinaldo, *Atheists, Agnostics, and Deists in America* (Briarcliff Manor, N.Y: DorPete Press, 2000), p. 27.

before and during Jayne, *Jefferson's Declaration of Independence*, p. 40.

18 *Your reason* Thomas Jefferson, *Letter to Peter Carr,* August 10, 1787 (New York: Franklin Library ed.), pp. 350–351.

21 *our civil rights* Thomas Jefferson, *An Act for Establishing Religious Freedom* (New York: Franklin Library ed.), p. 254.

22 *instead . . . of putting*   Thomas Jefferson, *Notes on the State of Virginia* (New York: Franklin Library ed.), p. 212.

23 *imaginary thing*   Thomas Paine, *The Age of Reason* (New York: Citadel, 1974), p. 186.

uncompromising belief   Willard Sterne Randall, *Thomas Jefferson: A Life* (New York: Henry Holt, 1993), pp. 85–86.

liberated him and *To him it was not sufficient*   Jayne, *Jefferson's Declaration of Independence*, p. 106.

24 *infidel*   Randall, *Thomas Jefferson*, p. 543.

it does me no injury   Ibid.

doubted the reality and *sinned in questioning*   Ibid.

the day will come   Jayne, *Jefferson's Declaration of Independence*, p. 34.

25 *the mystical and*   Charles B. Sanford, *The Religious Life of Thomas Jefferson* (Charlottesville: University Press of Virginia, 1984), p. 147.

This story is upon   Paine, *The Age of Reason*, p. 157.

26 *It is, however*   Ibid., pp. 52–53.

the theory of what is called   Ibid., p. 53.

a direct incorporation   Ibid.

27 *trinity of gods*   Ibid.

Of all the systems   Ibid., p.186.

The Christian theory   Ibid., p. 53.

the Bible and the Testament   Ibid., pp. 168–169.

28 *carry no internal evidence*   Ibid., p. 52.

such as any man   Ibid.

that God visits   Ibid.

Where did we get   Jayne, *Jefferson's Declaration of Independence*, p. 34.

29 *the stupidity of some*   Church, "Foreword," in Jefferson, *The Jefferson Bible*, p. 28.

a groundwork of vulgar   Ibid, p. 29.

the real villain   Pelikan, "Afterword," in Jefferson, *The Jefferson Bible*, p. 153.

the greatest of all   Ibid., p. 156.

30 *It is not to be understood*   Church, "Foreword," in Jefferson, *The Jefferson Bible*, p. 27.

genuine . . . doctrines   Thomas Jefferson, *Letter to William Short*, October 31, 1819 (New York: Franklin Library ed.), p. 556.

pleasure is the beginning   Rinaldo, *Atheists, Agnostics, and Deists in America*, p. 7.

that a hedonistic   Jayne, *Jefferson's Declaration of Independence*, p. 135.

the immaculate conception   Jefferson, *Letter to William Short*, October 31, 1819 (New York: Franklin Library ed.), p. 557.

31 *incomprehensible, unintelligible*   Sanford, *The Religious Life*, p. 90.

He revered the writings   Ibid, pp. 89–90.

in the existence   Ibid., p. 145.

concept of "being saved" [Jefferson's disbelief]   Ibid., p. 169.

or in "grace" [Jefferson's disbelief]   Jayne, *Jefferson's Declaration of Independence*, p. 172.

influenced by the Roman   Sanford, *The Religious Life*, p. 142.

it was a prime article   Ibid., p. 144.

unconnected system   Church, "Foreword," in Jefferson, *The Jefferson Bible*, p. 5.

defective as a whole   Ibid., p. 11.

writings of ancient   Ibid., p. 5.

32 *always in alliance*   Jayne, *Jefferson's Declaration of Independence*, pp. 137–138.

You may ask   Ibid., p. 141.

in the only sense   Thomas Jefferson, *Letter to Benjamin Rush*, April 21, 1803 (New York: Franklin Library ed.), p. 456.

In some of his private   Jefferson, *Letter to Benjamin Rush*, September 23, 1800 (New York: Franklin Library ed.), p. 449.

opposer of Christianity Isaac Kramnick and R. Laurence Moore, *The Godless Constitution: The Case against Religious Correctness* (New York: W.W. Norton, 1991), p. 89.

33 *a total disregard* Ibid., p. 92.

I rejoice that Jayne, *Jefferson's Declaration of Independence*, p. 166.

was not only in accord Ibid., pp. 166–167.

34 *in modern day parlance* Joseph J. Ellis, *American Sphinx: The Character of Thomas Jefferson* (New York: Alfred A. Knopf, 1997), p. 310.

the secularization of Jayne, *Jefferson's Declaration of Independence*, p. 99.

Federalist newspaper editors Rinaldo, *Atheists, Agnostics, and Deists in America*, p. 47.

35 *Dozens of pamphlets and articles* Sanford, *The Religious Life*, pp. 1–2.

filthy little atheist Rinaldo, *Atheists, Agnostics, and Deists in America*, p. 54.

was genuinely alarmed Editor's note in Paine, *The Age of Reason*, p. 47.

the belief in Stephen L. Carter, *The Culture of Disbelief* (New York: Anchor Books, 1994), p. 25.

36 *I hope for happiness* Paine, *The Age of Reason*, p. 50.

I content myself Ibid., p. 98.

A very numerous part Ibid., p. 178.

37 *we [shall] meet again* Sanford, *The Religious Life*, p. 157.

Some Jefferson scholars argue Ibid., p. 147.

As a student of law Ibid., p. 145.

faith which is not Jayne, *Jefferson's Declaration of Independence*, p. 39.

39 *Jefferson often wrote of the "pillow of ignorance"* Sanford, *The Religious Life*, p. 165.

He [Jesus], taught Jefferson, *Letter to Benjamin Rush*, April 21, 1803, in *Syllabus of an Estimate of the Merit of the*

Doctrines of Jesus, compared with those of others (New York: Franklin Library ed.), p. 459.

40 *That which is despicable* Babylonian Talmud; Shabbat 31a.
To love God Sanford, *The Religious Life*, p. 127.

41 *I hold* Jayne, *Jefferson's Declaration of Independence*, p. 26.
Look around Rinaldo, *Atheists, Agnostics, and Deists in America*, pp. 20–21.

42 *The reality is* Alan Dershowitz, *Shouting Fire: Civil Liberties in a Tumultuous Age* (Boston: Little, Brown, 2002), p. 11.

45 *a magisterium outside of science* See generally: Stephen Jay Gould, *Rocks of Ages: Science and Religion in the Fullness of Life* (New York: Ballantine Pub. Group, 1999).

51 *made no effort* Pelikan, "Afterword," in Jefferson, *The Jefferson Bible*, p. 159.
Religion [is] a subject Church, "Foreword," in Jefferson, *The Jefferson Bible*, p.22.

52 *and when thou prayest* Jefferson, *The Jefferson Bible*, pp. 49–50.
I am moreover and *questions of faith* Jefferson, *Letter to Benjamin Rush*, April 21, 1803 (New York: Franklin Library ed.), pp. 456–457.
to proclaim a national Sanford, *The Religious Life*, p. 2.
was thrilled in 1818 Kramnick, *The Godless Constitution*, p. 99
opposition to any form Sanford, *The Religious Life*, p. 3.

53 *religion was a* Randall, *Thomas Jefferson*, p. 291.
laws made for the Jews Jayne, *Jefferson's Declaration of Independence*, p. 30.
reading of the Bible Jefferson, *Notes on the State of Virginia* (New York: Franklin Library ed.), p. 221.

54 *produced the first* Randall, *Thomas Jefferson*, p. 28.
preserve the wall Kramnick, *The Godless Constitution*, p. 98.

55 *civil authority* Ibid.

I hope to see ADL, *The Religious Right,* pp. 4–6.

56 *Over the years* Sanford, *The Religious Life,* p. 2.

57 *is a matter* Thomas Jefferson, *To a Committee of the Danbury Baptist Association,* January 11, 1802 (New York: Franklin Library ed.), p. 269.

In truth Jefferson, "Appendix," in *Reports of Cases Determined in the General Courts of Virginia,* p. 142.

58 *It is certain* Paine, *The Age of Reason,* p. 98.

59 *He was even reticent* Sanford, *The Religious Life,* p. 147.

anticlerical and *rejected the moral* Jayne, *Jefferson's Declaration of Independence,* p. 63.

history . . . furnishes no example Ibid., p. 101.

bias against institutionalized Ibid., pp. 149–150.

The Jews excited Sanford, *The Religious Life,* p. 26.

61 *May it [the Declaration of Independence] be to the world* Jefferson, *Letter to Roger C. Weightman,* June 24, 1826 (New York: Franklin Library ed.), p. 585.

elects some of his creatures Jayne, *Jefferson's Declaration of Independence,* p. 36.

I can never join Ibid., p. 37.

62 *theology born* Ibid., p. 174.

saw the concepts Ibid., p. 7.

heterodox theology and *is institutionalized* Ibid.

see no constitutional problem *Edwards* v. *Aguillard,* 482 U.S. 578, 606–607.

64 *Indeed, the Declaration* Pfeffer, *Church, State, and Freedom,* pp. 209–210.

a [proposed] reference to Christ Ibid., p. 208.

the government of the United States Ibid., p. 211.

65 *No civil state* Ibid., p. 76.

Franklin described himself Rinaldo, *Atheists, Agnostics, and Deists in America,* pp. 34–36.

reject[ed] his Christian Edmund S. Morgan, *Benjamin Franklin* (New Haven: Yale University Press, 2002), p. 29.

never came to accept Ibid., p. 19.

66 *At one point he expressed*   Ibid., p. 19.
   ridiculed the idea   Ibid., p. 21.
   John Adams, too   Rinaldo, *Atheists, Agnostics, and Deists in America*, pp. 40–41.
   The Priesthood have   Ibid., p. 48.
67 *spirit of dogmatism*   McCullough, *John Adams*, p. 37.
   reason, to find, our nobler powers, and *the real design*   Ibid., p. 42.
   The question before   Rinaldo, *Atheists, Agnostics, and Deists in America*, p. 49.
68 *I do not like*   John Adams, *Letter to Thomas Jefferson*, May 5, 1816.
   Can a free government   Adams, *Letter to Thomas Jefferson*, May 19, 1821.
   there is not   Church, "Preface," in Jefferson, *The Jefferson Bible*, p. ix.
69 *cast[ing] aspersions*   McCullough, *John Adams*, p. 113.
   You rose and defended   Ibid., pp. 113–114.
   daring to the point   George Dangerfield, *Chancellor Robert R. Livingston of New York (1784–1813)* (New York: Harcourt, Brace, 1960), p. 293.
   In any event, only Jefferson   Carl Becker, *The Declaration of Independence* (New York: Vintage, 1958), p. 152.
70 *since Congress sat*   Becker, *The Declaration of Independence*, p. 171.
   Once again the curtain fell   Maier, *American Scripture*, p. 143.
71 *expression of the American*   Jefferson, *Letter to Henry Lee*, May 8, 1825 (New York: Franklin Library ed.), p. 577.
   My opinion on   Jayne, *Jefferson's Declaration of Independence*, p. 116.
72 *saw the importance*   Sanford, *The Religious Life*, p. 145.
   What really aroused   Ibid., p. 146.
   When great evils happen   Sanford, *The Religious Life*, p. 155.
73 *It is reasonable*   Pfeffer, *Church, State, and Freedom*, p. 208.

no religious test   Kramnick, *The Godless Constitution*, p. 29.

The entire Constitution   Ibid., p. 22.

74 *Americans, in the era*   Ibid., p. 17.

Religious indifference   Kramnick, *The Godless Constitution*, p. 17.

churches would have   Ibid.

In a general way   Ibid.

were the accepted premises   Becker, *The Declaration of Independence*, p. 26.

75 *Omission of reference to God*   Pfeffer, *Church, State, and Freedom*, pp. 209–210.

80 *bad science*   Carter, *The Culture of Disbelief*, p. 161.

sinful and tyrannical   Jefferson, *An Act Establishing Religious Freedom* (New York: Franklin Library ed.), p. 253.

82 *I have sworn*   Kramnick, *The Godless Constitution*, p. 68.

enduring commitment   Ibid.

83 *I promised you*   Jefferson, *Letter to Benjamin Rush*, September 23, 1800 (New York: Franklin Library ed.), p. 449.

84 *Jefferson was not*   Kramnick, *The Godless Constitution*, pp. 95–96.

2. WHAT ARE "THE LAWS OF NATURE AND OF NATURE'S GOD"?

89 *impressed on the sense*   Jayne, *Jefferson's Declaration of Independence*, p. 116.

State a moral case   Jefferson, *Letter to Peter Carr*, August 10, 1787 (New York: Franklin Library ed.), p. 349.

felt their rights   Jayne, *Jefferson's Declaration of Independence*, p. 117.

law in the nature   Ibid., p. 116.

as much a part of   Wills, *Inventing America*, p. 204.

90 *to ask whether*   Becker, *The Declaration of Independence*, p. 277.

91 *innate categories*   Ronald Dworkin, *Taking Rights Seriously*
   (Cambridge, Mass: Harvard University Press, 1978), p. 158.
   do not exercise   Ibid., p. 272.
92 *miracle, mystery*   Quoted in Alan Dershowitz, *Shouting
   Fire: Civil Liberties in a Turbulent Age* (Boston: Little,
   Brown, 2002), p. 56.
   nothing has been   Ibid.
   to build their tower   Ibid.
93 *Rights, to the extent*   Dworkin, *Taking Rights Seriously*,
   pp. 190–191, 269.
94 *In 1861, for example*   Ellis, "The Enduring Influence of
   the Declaration," in Ellis, *What Did the Declaration
   Declare*, p. 16.
96 *that the opinions*   Jefferson, *An Act for Establishing Religious Freedom* (New York: Franklin Library ed.), p. 254.
   Thomas Jefferson thought so   Dworkin, *Taking Rights Seriously*, p. 266.
97 *laws are needed*   Ibid., p. 267.
   in any strong sense   Ibid.
104 *though we well know*   Jefferson, *An Act for Establishing
   Religious Freedom*, pp. 254–255.
   to furnish contributions   Ibid.
   be free to profess   Ibid., p. 255.
105 *On the day*   Michael Paulson, "Catholics Reject Evange-
   lization of Jews," *Boston Globe*, August 13, 2002.
   God designed Bradwell v. State, 83 U.S. 130 (prior history).
106 *The paramount destiny   Bradwell v. State*, 83 U.S. 130,
   141 (Bradley, J., concurring).
   To be an advocate   Dershowitz, *Shouting Fire*, p. 10.
108 *The naturalistic fallacy*   Ibid., p. 495.
109 *nature's retribution*   Jeff Cohen and Norman Solomon,
   "Cosmo's deadly advice to women about AIDS" (*Seattle
   Times*, July 31, 1993).
   early relatives were monkeys   Keyes, address to the Declaration Foundation, 1996.

might makes right and *only for the strong*   Keyes, Virginia high school appearance, February 28, 2000.

110 *this is what our children learn*   Ibid.

a kind of intelligent and *dispensed with*   Ibid.

112 *And so once you have seen*   Keyes, address to the Declaration Foundation, 1996.

121 *He [King George III of Great Britain] has waged cruel war*   Becker, *The Declaration of Independence*, pp. 212–213.

3. HOW CAN JEFFERSON'S VIEWS OF EQUALITY AND SLAVERY BE RECONCILED?

123 *Mr. Jefferson attended*   Garry Wills, *Inventing America* (New York: Vintage, 1978), p. 13.

124 *At about the time*   William Cohen, "Thomas Jefferson and the Problem of Slavery," *Journal of American History,* vol. 56, no. 3 (1969), p. 506.

was of being carried and subsequent information in this paragraph   John C. Miller, *The Wolf by the Ears* (New York: Free Press, 1977), p. 1.

125 *deep-rooted prejudices*   Jefferson, *Notes on the State of Virginia* (New York: Franklin Library ed.), p. 206.

ten thousand recollections   Ibid.

new provocations and *the real distinctions*   Ibid.

convulsions which will probably   Ibid.

something is not done   Cohen, "Thomas Jefferson and the Problem of Slavery," p. 521.

126 *We have the wolf*   Miller, *The Wolf by the Ears,* frontispiece.

Jefferson was the intellectual godfather   Paul Finkelman, "Jefferson and Slavery," in *Jeffersonian Legacies,* ed. P. Onuf. (Charlottesville: University Press of Virginia, 1993), p. 186.

127 *The first difference*   Jefferson, *Notes on the State of Virginia* (New York: Franklin Library ed.), pp. 206–207.

128 *They seem to require*   Ibid., p. 207.

129 *Comparing them by*   Ibid.

It will be right Ibid., pp. 207–208. *See also* Henry Louis Gates Jr., "Phyllis Wheatley on Trial," *New Yorker,* January 20, 2003.

130 *it is not their condition* Ibid., p. 210.

apt to suspect the Negroes Wills, *Inventing America,* p. 219.

131 *I advance it* Jefferson, *Notes on the State of Virginia* (New York: Franklin Library ed.), p. 211.

Whether further observation Ibid., p. 210.

132 *That disposition to theft* Ibid.

the appointment of a woman Thomas Jefferson, *Letter to Albert Gallatan,* January 13, 1807.

133 *We believe the history* Sims v. Balkcom, 220 Ga. 7, pp. 11–12 (1964) (Duckworth, C.J.).

our culture takes reason Wills, *Inventing America,* p. 224.

Thus when Jefferson says Ibid., pp. 225–226.

134 *superior to others* Cohen, "Thomas Jefferson and the Problem of Slavery," pp. 507–508.

The entire body of Ibid., pp. 510.

It would seem hardly John Hope Franklin, *Racial Equality in America* (Chicago: University of Chicago Press, 1976), p. 19.

135 *My opinion has ever been* Wills, *Inventing America,* p. 300.

136 *The eradication of slavery* Miller, *The Wolf by the Ears,* p. 1.

negative, slaves we have, and *it is necessary* Cohen, "Thomas Jefferson and the Problem of Slavery," p. 507.

no person hereafter Ibid.

Miller even speculates Miller, *The Wolf by the Ears,* pp. 14–15.

137 *Jefferson was outraged* Ibid., p. 8.

138 *his Majesty's troops* Ibid., p. 10.

thought the expression Ibid., p. 9 (footnote).

John Jay revealed William W. Freehling, "The Founding Fathers and Slavery," *The American Historical Review,* vol. 77, no. 1 (1972), p. 86.

139 *the African trade*   Finkelman, "Jefferson and Slavery,"
     p. 192.
   the restricted supply   Freehling, "The Founding Fathers and
     Slavery," p. 89.
   Jefferson knew from his   Joseph J. Ellis, "The Spring of '76:
     Texts and Contexts," in Ellis, *What Did the Declaration
     Declare,* p. 86.
   jeopardized his political career   Finkelman, "Jefferson and
     Slavery," p. 186.
140 *I had him severely flogged*   Cohen, "Thomas Jefferson and
     the Problem of Slavery," p. 516.
   will never again serve   Ibid.
141 *Throughout his life*   Ibid.
   For information on Jefferson's runaways see Ibid., p. 515.
   nothing is more certainly   Wills, *Inventing America,* p.
     306.
142 *Neither did Jefferson show*   Cohen, "Thomas Jefferson and
     the Problem of Slavery," p. 509.
143 *feared that a sizable*   Ibid.
   it is high time we should face   Ibid., p. 520.
   never was so deep a tragedy   Ibid.
144 *To emancipate all slaves born*   Jefferson, *Notes on the State
     of Virginia* (New York: Franklin Library ed.), p. 206.
   practicable for us   Cohen, "Thomas Jefferson and the
     Problem of Slavery," p. 523.
   Their estimated value   Ibid., p. 524.
145 *nurture with the mother*   Ibid.
   It is certain and *that these two races*   Wills, *Inventing
     America,* p. 306.
146 *In the end, Jefferson's ideas*   Garrett Ward Sheldon, *The
     Political Philosophy of Thomas Jefferson* (Baltimore: Johns
     Hopkins University Press, 1991), p. 140.
147 *Slavery is the perfect*   Dershowitz, *Shouting Fire,* pp.
     22–25.

CONCLUSION

151 *the signs of our ideas only*   John Locke, *An Essay Concerning Human Understanding*, 1690.

152 *dead, the conventional fallacy,* and other quoted excepts in this paragraph   Antonin Scalia, "God's Justice and Ours," *First Things* (May 2002), p. 17.

158 *eternal, immutable laws*   Sir William Blackstone, *Commentaries*, sect. 2 (Law of Nature).

159 *The life of the law*   Oliver Wendell Holmes Jr., *The Common Law*, lecture 1 (1881).

162 *elective abortions* and other information in this paragraph   Zoila Acevedo, "Abortion in Early America," *Women and Health*, vol. 4 (1979), pp. 160–161.

163 *presaging the sentiments*   *Compassion in Dying* v. *State of Washington*, 79 F.3d 790, 846 (1996) (Beezer, J., dissenting).

Men are too much   Ibid.

if this is a "Christian Nation"   www.jesbeard.com/JeffersonQuotations.htm.

164 *Indeed, Jefferson's puritanical*   Randall, *Thomas Jefferson*, p. 299.

167 *the unbound exercise*   Jefferson, *Letter to Roger C. Weightman*, June 24, 1826 (New York: Franklin Library ed.), p. 585.

the history of American   Jayne, *Jefferson's Declaration of Independence*, p. 1.

Index

191

Printed in the USA
CPSIA information can be obtained
at www.ICGtesting.com
JSHW012028140824
68134JS00033B/2931